PLEASE RETURN THIS ITEM
BY THE DUE DATE TO ANY
TULSA CITY-COUNTY LIBRARY.

FINES ARE 5¢ PER DAY; A
MAXIMUM OF $1.00 PER ITEM.

RSAC

JUL ▮▮ 1995

Gaspara Stampa

Selected Poems

D0916512

Translation Copyright © 1994 by
Laura Anna Stortoni

ITALICA PRESS, INC.
595 Main Street
New York, New York 10044

All rights reserved. No part of this publication may be reproduced, stored in a retrieval system, or transmitted, in any form or by any means, electronic, mechanical, photocopying, recording, or otherwise, without prior permission of Italica Press.

Library of Congress Cataloging-in-Publication Data
Stampa, Gaspara, ca. 1523-ca. 1554.
    [Selections. English & Italian. 1994]
    Selected poems / edited and translated by Laura Anna Stortoni &
Mary Prentice Lillie.
        p. cm.
    Includes bibliographical references and index.
    ISBN 0-934977-37-2 : $15.00
    1. Stampa, Gaspara, ca. 1523-ca. 1554—Translations into English.
I. Stortoni, Laura Anna, 1942- . II. Lillie, Mary Prentice. III. Title.
PQ4634.S65A27 1994
851'.4—dc20   94-30764
                                                      CIP

Cover Illustration: Portrait of a Young Lady, Antonio Pollaiuolo, Staatliche Museen zu Berlin – Preußischer Kulturbesitz Gemäldegalerie. Foto: Jörg P. Anders

Printed in the United States of America
5 4 3 2 1

Gaspara Stampa

Selected Poems

Edited and Translated by
Laura Anna Stortoni
&
Mary Prentice Lillie

ITALICA PRESS
NEW YORK
1994

Translation Copyright © 1994 by
Laura Anna Stortoni

ITALICA PRESS, INC.
595 Main Street
New York, New York 10044

All rights reserved. No part of this publication may be reproduced,
stored in a retrieval system, or transmitted, in any form or by any
means, electronic, mechanical, photocopying, recording, or other-
wise, without prior permission of Italica Press.

Library of Congress Cataloging-in-Publication Data
Stampa, Gaspara, ca. 1523-ca. 1554.
    [Selections. English & Italian. 1994]
    Selected poems / edited and translated by Laura Anna Stortoni &
Mary Prentice Lillie.
        p. cm.
    Includes bibliographical references and index.
    ISBN 0-934977-37-2 : $15.00
    1. Stampa, Gaspara, ca. 1523-ca. 1554—Translations into English.
I. Stortoni, Laura Anna, 1942- . II. Lillie, Mary Prentice. III. Title.
PQ4634.S65A27 1994
851'.4—dc20   94-30764
                                                  CIP

Cover Illustration: Portrait of a Young Lady, Antonio Pollaiuolo,
Staatliche Museen zu Berlin – Preußischer Kulturbesitz
Gemäldegalerie. Foto: Jörg P. Anders

Printed in the United States of America
5 4 3 2 1

851.4 S783g 1994
Stampa, Gaspara,
Gaspara Stampa :

ABOUT THE EDITORS

LAURA ANNA STORTONI was born in Italy and educated in Europe and the U.S. (B.A., M.A., and Ph.D. candidate in Comparative Literature, University of California, Berkeley). She has published her poetry and poetry translations in several major magazines and journals. She has also co-edited with Mary Prentice Lillie *Women Poets of the Italian Renaissance: Courtly Ladies and Courtesans* (Italica Press, 1995). She has just completed a volume of her own poetry with an introduction by Diane di Prima. She has translated the poetry of Giuseppe Conte *(The Ocean and the Boy)*. She is now at work on an anthology of Italian women poets of the twentieth century, *The Pomegranate*.

MARY PRENTICE LILLIE was educated at Vassar and at the University of California, Berkeley (Ph.D. in English) and has authored a verse translation of *The Divine Comedy* (San Francisco: Grabhorn Press, 1958), and several volumes of her own poetry: *Epiphanies* (1965), *A Decade of Dreams* (1979), and *Times and Seasons* (1986). She has also authored *A Desperate Character,* a biography of her mother, the philanthropist Francis Crane. She is presently completing a poetic diary, *Gifts of Fate*.

TULSA CITY-COUNTY LIBRARY

Contents

CHRONOLOGY

1523   Gaspara Stampa is born in Padua.

1530   Death of Stampa's father, Bartolomeo.

1531   Stampa's mother, Cecilia, moves with her three children to her native Venice.

1544   Death of Stampa's only brother, Baldassarre.

1548   Stampa meets Collaltino di Collalto at Christmas time.

1549   Collaltino leaves for France to fight against the English in the service of Henry II, king of France. In November, Collaltino returns to Venice for a few months and takes up his relationship with Stampa again.

1550   Collaltino leaves again. Stampa becomes a member of the *Accademia dei Dubbiosi* under the name of "Anaxilla." Toward the end of the year Collaltino again returns to Venice, and Stampa spends time with him at his estate, but by the end of the year, deeply depressed, she returns to Venice, marking the end of her relationship with Collaltino and the beginning of a new relationship with Bartolomeo Zen.

1551-52   With improving health, Stampa enjoys a period of relative tranquility.

1553   Stampa's health worsens, and she spends a few months in Florence hoping that the milder climate may cure her.

1554   Stampa returns to Venice, becomes ill with a high fever, and after fifteen days she dies on April 23. The register of her parish notes that she died of fever and colic, and of *mal de mare* (Venetian literally for disease of the matrix). In October, Pietrasanta publishes the first edition of Stampa's poetry, edited by her sister Cassandra and dedicated to Monsignor della Casa.

INTRODUCTION

Gaspara Stampa (1523-1554) is generally regarded by most critics as not only the greatest woman poet of the Italian Renaissance, but also as the greatest Italian woman poet ever. She forms part of the traditional triptych of Italian Renaissance women poets, along with Veronica Gambara (1485-1550) and Vittoria Colonna (1492-1547); but she surpasses her courtly predecessors for poetic originality. She has also been one of the most controversial Italian women poets. "Was she a courtesan or not?" is the question – still unresolved – that has busied many critics.

Scholars have attempted to reconstruct her life on the basis of sparse biographical evidence, taking poetic and literary statements in her work at historical face value, and using their imaginations rather freely. Whatever her status may have been during her lifetime, for her passionate and intense temperament she remains the most forceful and original of all Italian woman poets, and – thanks perhaps to her talent and training as a musician – she produced some of the most musical poetry in the Italian language.[1]

In tribute to her capacity to sublimate real-life experience, with its joys and sorrows, Rainer Maria Rilke, in the first of his *Duino Elegies*, remembers her thus:

> But Nature, spent and exhausted, takes lovers back
> into herself, as if there were not enough strength
> to create them a second time. Have you imagined
> Gaspara Stampa intensely enough so that any girl
> deserted by her beloved might be inspired
> by that fierce example of soaring, objectless love
> and might say to herself, "Perhaps I can be like her"?
> Shouldn't this most ancient of sufferings finally grow
> more fruitful for us? Isn't it time that we lovingly
> freed ourselves from the beloved and, quivering, endured:
> as the arrow endures the bowstring's tension, so that
> gathered in the snap of release it can be more than
> itself. For there is no place where we can remain.[2]

Stampa was born in 1523 in Padua, of a noble Milanese family in decline. Her mother, Cecilia, originally from Venice, also came from a good family. Gaspara had a sister, Cassandra, and a brother, Baldassarre. For financial reasons, Gaspara's father Bartolomeo became a jeweler, but he died c.1530, leaving his family to fend for itself. Cecilia decided to return to her native Venice, where, in a more intellectual and artistic atmosphere, she brought up her three children with an excellent education – including Greek, Latin, rhetoric, music, and literature – that equalled the education given to the children of aristocratic families in those days.[3] The Stampa family took lodgings in the parish of the Saints Gervasio and Protasio, which is now San Trovaso. While all three of the Stampa children had the benefit of being taught by some of the best tutors of the time in the sciences and literature, the two girls were also taught by the famous French musician and composer Perissone Cambio, who trained them in both lute and voice. Thanks to the precocious talents of her children, the house of Cecilia Stampa became a literary and musical center. From 1535 to 1540, it was the gathering place for musicians and literati, including Francesco Sansovino, son of the great Florentine architect Jacopo, Lodovico Domenichi, Girolamo Parabosco, the humanist physician Ortensio Lando, the scholars Sperone Speroni and Benedetto Varchi, and many others.

Of the two sisters, Gaspara was the more talented; Cassandra, although a good musician in her own right, remained overshadowed by Gaspara's brilliance, but together the two sisters delighted the company with their conversation, their madrigals, and their singing of Petrarch's poems while accompanying themselves on the lute. They enjoyed the freedom of movement and expression that their artistic profession permitted them. However, it was a freedom that perhaps cost them their reputations and that has caused many critics to speculate whether they belonged to the throng of courtesans that existed and, indeed, flourished in Venice at the time. The critic A. Salza, who published the critical edition[4] of Stampa's *Rime* together with that of the courtesan Veronica Franco (1546-1591), tried without success to find conclusive evidence that Stampa had been a courtesan. The truth is that, like many free-spirited women, Stampa and her sister may have been much maligned. Nevertheless, a letter survives that was written to Stampa by her relative, Suor Angelica Paola de' Negri, abbess of the Convent of San Paolo in Milan, begging Stampa to make sure that the *conversazioni* (social gatherings) did not endanger her "beautiful virtue."

Benedetto Croce, who had a special appreciation of her poetry, referred to her as *l'appassionata,* the passionate woman, who was "not a courtesan by trade, as some contemporaries classified her, but certainly a woman outside the rules, probably a *virtuosa* of music and singing, with the free and easy attitudes toward life and the egalitarian relationships that the [musical] profession entailed and almost justified."[5]

In 1544, at the age of 19, young Baldassarre Stampa, who had shown great promise as a poet, died, possibly of tuberculosis. The young man was greatly admired by his friend Francesco Sansovino, who wrote about him in the dedication of his *Ragionamenti d'amore*[6] to Gaspara Stampa. The death of the much-beloved brother triggered in Stampa a deep religious crisis, and, as documented in her correspondence with Suor Angelica, she considered abandoning mundane pursuits for the peace of the cloister. Stampa isolated herself for some time.

In the meantime, her fame grew, and, in addition to the *Ragionamenti,* Sansovino dedicated to her a reprint of Boccaccio's *Ameto* and *Lettura di Benedetto Varchi sopra un sonetto di Monsignor della Casa.* More artists flocked to the Stampa salon, among them the painter

Tiepolo and Giorgio Benzone. Her teacher, Perissone Cambio, wrote of her musical talent, "No lady in the world loves music more than she, and none has a rarer degree of mastery over it." He added, addressing her directly, that there were "thousands upon thousands of gentle and noble spirits who have heard your sweet harmonies and have given you the name of heavenly siren."7

There seems to be evidence that Stampa had been in love before the age of twenty-six, when her famous liaison with Collaltino di Collalto, count of Treviso, began. Stampa was at the height of her musical career and was greatly admired for her charm and voice. Nevertheless, she described herself as falling in love with Collaltino when she was "incautious," "young," and "unaware," which may not have been exactly the case. It must have been true, however, that Collaltino was her first great passion, and the most consuming one of her life. Precisely, as she records in Poem 2, around Christmas time in 1548, in the salon of Domenico Venier, she met him and fell passionately in love with him at first sight. An anonymous poem of Stampa's time, written by one of her detractors, states that, before meeting Collaltino, Stampa had been the mistress of a certain Gritti, "who had her first." He was possibly a well-known person, since he is characterized as *il Gritti*. But, attempting to indicate a new beginning for herself, Stampa described how this love for Collaltino nested in her at Christmas time, just as Christ had nested in Mary's womb. She is obviously using this figure to evoke both a symbolic virginity and the visceral quality of her love.

Collaltino was the same age as she and was a patrician of some literary taste and a patron of the arts: Ortensio Lando's *I paradossi* were written and published under his patronage. He had a patrician sense of social superiority and appears, from the idealized portrait that survives, exactly as Stampa described him: handsome, but a little haughty and disdainful.[8] Although he had been trained for arms more than for arts, Collaltino also wrote some poetry and had literary friendships with Pietro Aretino, Girolamo Muzio, Lodovico Domenichi and other important scholars of the time. His own secretary was Giuseppe Betussi, a young *literato* who wrote a famous dialogue on love, the *Raverta*. When, at the beginning of their relationship, Stampa started to shower Collaltino with sonnets, he gallantly attempted to reciprocate, but he was not particularly gifted, and his sonnets – some of which are published in Salza's critical edition of Stampa's *Rime* – are stiff, artificial, and devoid of originality. Stampa was not totally blinded by love. In "Why do you waste…" (117), while seemingly declaring herself as an unworthy object of his rhymes, she told him between the lines that he should *not* write, but that he should let *her* celebrate *him*. Collaltino was to be cast in the role of Beatrice or Laura.

The liaison with Collaltino lasted, on and off, three years – years that marked a deep transformation in Stampa's life and changed the direction of her talent from that of a musician and *cantatrice* to a poet who used her new inspiration to write the poems that form her love diary. If we are to judge by these poems, the relationship between Stampa and Collaltino was far from happy. While in several poems she sang the praise of Collaltino and sang of her own happiness, a far larger number of poems describe her loneliness, bereavement, jealousy, and humiliation. During this relationship, Stampa experienced the extremes of joy and despair, and even while she was at his side, she was always insecure (56); and the worm of jealousy (155), she wrote, always gnawed at her heart (187).

While that blond patrician was at first flattered by the overt attentions of such an admired and talented woman, in the long run he may have become irked by Stampa's intensity, which he could not reciprocate or match in any way. Maybe Collaltino was overwhelmed. Stampa's jealousy and vehemence – as witnessed in her poetry – must have severely restricted his free and easy life-style. Moreover, this proud patrician must have been troubled by a sense of inadequacy and unbalance in the relationship with such a powerful and talented woman. He is a little cold, she wrote, a little fickle, a little disdainful. But precisely because Collaltino was made cold by the Moon (4), precisely because Collaltino was passive and elusive, Stampa loved him so much – she who admittedly despised those who loved her and loved those who fled from her. If Stampa needed a poetic and emotional challenge, Collaltino provided it.

If it is true that in every love there is a lover and a beloved, and that the lover is more important than the beloved, Stampa certainly took the leading role in her relationship with Collaltino, and he remained no more than the object of her passion, whose existence was to provide the emotion and inspiration for her muse.

The beginning of her relationship with Collaltino – placed at Christmas in either a mystical or contrived coincidence – signified for her a new birth; and Stampa then began her love diary, which was modeled in many ways after Petrarch's poems for Laura and echoed many Petrarchan themes, reelaborated in an original manner. Now, however, the poetic tables were turned, and it was the lady who celebrated the lord's beauty and sang his praises.

Stampa seriously started to write to record specifically every nuance of her feelings, every detail of her amorous Calvary. Her collected poems have a narrative thread, loose as it may be, and, as in Petrarch's poems, each one marks a milestone of her love. But, while she worked within the Petrarchan tradition – which was almost obligatory for a lyric poet of that time – she transcended its limits with her original and tempestuous nature. Her musical education and exceptional ear equipped her to write highly musical verses, and at the same time she disdained too much polishing, too much melodiousness. Her passion was aggressive, and the verses expressing it were direct and forceful. Also the persona she chose to assume in the love-story was "masculine":

she was the pursuer, she was the hunter. Collaltino was the beloved object, the target for her love and her intensity, which were immediately sublimated into art.

Stampa's poetry reveals that there was a deep social context to her love for Collaltino, which was metaphorically expressed in her beloved's name, Collalto, "high hill." Stampa, no matter how much she was admired, wooed, or appreciated, did not belong to the aristocracy and was without real nobility and rank. In the past, the Stampa family had been noble and wealthy, so Stampa's attempted ascent of the "high hill" of Collaltino's family was also, in some sense, a return to the paradise of a lost status. In an age when it was virtually impossible for a woman to change her social standing, except by marriage, Stampa attempted to elevate herself through her art, through her talent. It is clear that "the high hill" also stood for the heights of the mythical Parnassus and Helicon, symbolizing the poetic glory that Stampa strove to reach.

Stampa, in her poetry, often called her beloved "Count" (98), seeming to enjoy the repetition of this title, and she claimed that she was "low" (8) and not worthy of Collaltino (150). However, through her poetry, Stampa not only elevated herself to Collaltino's level, but soared above it to reach high poetic peaks. Sonnet 3, although not in itself particularly felicitous, is important as a statement of intention: such love, painful as it may be, ennobles her and elevates her, "wakes up in her soul such talent!"

We should not take at face value Stampa's assertions about her low worth; rather, her repeated claims of inferiority should be seen as rhetorical devices serving to direct a brighter spotlight on the poet's excellence. While Stampa seemingly sets out to celebrate Collaltino, in reality she continues to extol herself as his moral and artistic superior. "The scales are not equal" (150), she writes, unable to deny the social chasm between herself and Collaltino. He is a patrician, his castle symbolically perched on a lofty hill. She is "an abject, low-born woman" (8). Yet, throughout her poetry Stampa never attempted to establish *equality* with her lover. Instead, she begins from an acknowledged position of inferiority by birth and, skipping the plane of equality, she reaches a self-declared position of superiority. Is she celebrating Collaltino or competing with him? Indeed, she relentlessly measured her talent, her steadfastness, her fidelity, and the depth of her emotions against Collaltino's fickle, weak, unfaithful, somewhat cold nature. Madrigal 235, for instance, ends with the emphatic juxtaposition: "O what a cruel lord! O what a loyal lady!" And in Poem 98, she claims moral superiority by virtue of the pain she has suffered for him: "My Count, your valor is so infinite/... But truly it's inferior to the pain/ that I have suffered through my love for you." For the most part, Stampa's comments on her worthlessness are filled with a subtle irony, which may well not have been perceived at the time. Far from being modest and servile, she knew full well, at all times, that she was a great artist, that by her art she was gaining fame for herself, and that she would be remembered by posterity, boldly exclaiming in Poem 91, "I alone conquer infinity!"

When Stampa, in Poem 132, complains to Love about her sufferings, the answer is that the purpose of that painful love is her art: "Let this suffice you, that it makes you write." As the love story described in her poetic diary progresses, the fatal equation *pena-penna* (pain-pen) is more and more prominent: the poetess feeds on pain as pain feeds her inspiration. Collaltino was a noble warrior and wielded the sword. Stampa wielded the pen, and in Italian pen and feather are the same word, *penna.* So with her pen Stampa soared high, like a strong, feathered bird, an eagle or a dove (13). Stampa realized that her pen gave her enormous powers, powers to reach far and wide, in the present and in the future. With her pen she could attain the fame that had not been hers by birth or marriage. With her pen she could reach Collaltino, she could overcome Collaltino's sword. And, more importantly, she could become the author of her own myth, a myth that stands the test of time. And, since pain was the ink that made her pen flow, pain was accepted, even welcomed. Stampa makes this concept – that is, the utility of pain for the purpose of artistic production – even clearer in her own preface to her poetry, which we have included in this book. While dedicating her poems to Collaltino, Stampa points out that "these fruits of love [her poems] have issued" from his "harshness" towards her. She does not berate him, however, declaring to Collaltino: "even in tormenting me you are beneficial and produce fruit."

In 1549, Collaltino went to France to fight under Henry II, king of France, for Boulogne-sur-Mer. She vainly attempted to persuade him to stay, and, after his departure, she wrote him many letters and love poems. He almost never answered her, causing her deep distress. Nevertheless, when he announced his return to Venice, Stampa was overjoyed ("With what sufficient greetings…" [101]), and sang of their reunion in one of her most celebrated sonnets, "O night…" (104), in which she acknowledged their intimacy with a frankness that was unusual for the time and may have contributed to the perception that she was a courtesan.

The liaison with Collaltino was rekindled. Although Stampa was not happy, she still could not live without her obsessive love. Her *voluptas dolendi*, her masochism, has often been remarked – especially in Poems 43 and 232 – as well as her willingness to endure countless rebuffs and humiliations and to accept for a relatively long time a painful and humiliating situation. Reading the original Italian text, one is struck by how often the word *martire* (and plural *martiri*) occurs. Stampa sees herself as a martyr for love; but she does not avoid martyrdom, actually welcomes it, since she is aware that with the martyrdom comes apotheosis. Stampa suffered but declared that the "torments caused by love are always blest" (24), and that suffering for Collaltino was better than rejoicing with someone else.[9] Stampa felt a deep attachment precisely to the one who neglected her, and she was unable to detach herself from Collaltino and from the pain he caused. However, a woman of Stampa's strength and character could not for long tolerate a relationship that left her with such a deep sense of unhappiness. First came depression, then revolt, eloquently expressed in the vehement, almost violent outbursts of poetic anger she vented towards her lover.

A few months after their reunion, Collaltino returned to France to distinguish himself in the war against England. He was to stay away until 1550. During this time Stampa often wrote to and about him, and she seems to have suffered deeply from jealousy of the women of the French court. Also, possibly at this time, she was accepted into the *Accademia dei Dubbiosi*,[10] and, significantly enough, she chose as her literary name "Anaxilla" (Anassilla is the Italianate form), from *Anaxum*, the Latin name of the river Piave, which flowed through the lands of the Collalto estate. Afterwards she often referred to herself as the "faithful and wretched Anaxilla"; and under that name she showered Collaltino with poems filled with passion and longing, as well as with tirades and reproaches, calling him cruel, disloyal, and impious.

We have evidence that long before they were collected and published, Stampa's poems circulated and were read and admired in Venetian salons. The madrigals were surely performed and sung. Thus, the literary story became well-known and started to run parallel to the love story. Stampa's poems – possibly initiated to ease the poet's sorrow – acquired the awesome power of public celebration, but even more of public accusation: Stampa did not languish in silence; she published her grievances loud and clear.

When Collaltino returned to Venice in 1550, he spent some time with Stampa at his castle of San Salvatore near Treviso. But soon Stampa's health worsened, and the poet sank into a deep depression.[11] The relationship finally ended. Stampa spent some time resting and recovering. Immediately after the break-up, she was both afraid of love and eager to fall in love again. She described herself as a salamander (208) – the mythical creature who could only live in fire. She was both weary of pain and addicted to it, and love was the fatal fire towards which she, *volontariamente,* of her own free will, moved.

The poet started – we do not know exactly when – a new relationship with the Venetian patrician Bartolomeo Zen. Although it lacked the intensity of her relationship with Collaltino, it was built on common interests and mutual respect. Between 1551 and 1552, Stampa enjoyed a calm and peaceful period. She was in good health, again surrounded by friends and admirers, and devotedly loved by Zen. In 1553, however, she became ill once more, and went to Florence to recover in a drier and milder climate.

It is not clear from what disease Stampa suffered. However, it seems to be out of the question that she died of poison; and the story of her alleged suicide after

Collaltino married, told by Antonio Rambaldo di Collalto in his preface to the edition of her poetry that he commissioned, is only a legend, for Collaltino married the noblewoman Giulia Torelli three years after Stampa's death. In her thirty-first year, Stampa died in Venice, fifteen days after her return from Florence. The death register of her parish reports the date as April 23, 1554.

In October of the same year, in Venice, Pietrasanta published the first edition of Gaspara Stampa's *Rime*. It was edited by her sister Cassandra and dedicated to Monsignor Della Casa. This was the only edition of her *Rime* until Collaltino's descendant Antonio Rambaldo commissioned Luisa Bargalli to edit the *Rime* again in 1738.

The apex of irony, and perhaps of poetic justice, is that it was precisely one of Collaltino's descendents who took the initiative of rescuing Stampa's poetry from the obscurity into which two centuries of silence had plunged them and had them published in a beautiful and impressive edition. Blind to Stampa's irony and insensitive to her grief, he believed – as evidenced by his own preface – that Stampa's *Rime* were an outright celebration of Collaltino. Deeply proud that his ancestor had been loved by so great an artist, Antonio Rambaldo, in fact, became in great part responsible for the perpetuation of Collatino's portrayal as the neglectful lover of a great woman poet.

Collaltino was a warrior. Stampa was a *virtuosa* and a poet. He went to war to acquire fame for himself through his exploits. She acquired great fame hardly stirring from Venice. During her life, she seemed prophetically aware of the fact that Collaltino's name would be remembered by posterity only by virtue of her pen. He strove to acquire glory for himself. But – and this is Stampa's tremendous posthumous revenge – he is remembered only as *she* portrays him: as an aloof, cold, and neglectful lover. His side of the story will never reach us, since he wrote little, and what little he wrote he did not write well.

Stampa, famous and celebrated in her days, was forgotten for a couple of centuries, until the 1738 re-editing of her poems. After that, she consistently enjoyed great favor. She was greatly beloved by Romantic critics and readers for her willingness to reveal her feelings, for the subtle psychological study to which she subjected herself, and for her spontaneous freedom of expression. Regrettably, however, Stampa's poetry was overshadowed by the vicissitudes of her love affairs. The facts of the poet's life were sensationalized, and, as her figure acquired legendary proportions, she became the subject of novels, plays, debates, and quarrels. Until recent critical re-evaluation, she was portrayed simply as a naive and tragic victim of love, but, in reality, she was, at all times, a true artist, fully aware of her poetic goals and fully conscious of the value of her endeavors.

From her poetry (208), the poet Gabriele D'Annunzio extracted the verse that he used as a motto: *"Viver ardendo e non sentire il male,"* to live burning and not to feel the pain.

— Laura Anna Stortoni
Berkeley, California
July 1994

NOTES

1. This introduction does not purport to offer an in-depth critical and scholarly study on Stampa's work, rather it is meant to provide the reader with sufficient background material to understand and appreciate the translated poems, and at the same time to offer the translators' interpretation of Stampa's work. For an exhaustive study of Stampa's life and works in English, we refer the reader to Fiora Bassanese, *Gaspara Stampa* (Boston: Twayne, 1982).

2. Rainer Maria Rilke, *The Selected Poetry,* ed. & trans. by Stephen Mitchell (New York: Vintage, 1989), 153. Rilke also mentioned Gaspara Stampa in his novel, *The Notebooks of Malte Laurids Brigge* (trans. by Stephen Mitchell [New York: Vintage, 1985], 134, 235), where the hero referred to Stampa as "One of those powerful examples of women in love, who, even while they called out to him, surpassed the man they loved, who did not cease until their torment turned into a bitter, icy magnificence." And again: "Women like Stampa hurl themselves after the man they have lost, but with their first steps they overtake him, and in front of them there is only God."

3. For details of Stampa's education, and for study of the education of girls in Stampa's times, see Bassanese, *Stampa,* ch. 1.

4. *Rime di Gaspara Stampa e di Veronica Franco* (Bari: Laterza, 1913).

5. *Poesia popolare e poesia d'arte* (Bari: Laterza, 1967), 369.

6. Francesco Sansovino, *Ragionamento nel quale brevemente s'insegna ai giovani la bella arte d'amore* (Venice: n.p., 1545).

7. A. Einstein, *The Italian Madrigal* (Princeton: Princeton University Press, 1971), 1:439.

8. The extant idealized portraits of Gaspara Stampa and Collaltino, originally contained in the edition commissioned in 1738 by Antonio Rambaldo di Collalto, are now in Milan, at the Civica Raccolta di Stampe Bertarelli. A reproduction and detailed description of these two portraits, in which Stampa appears as a muse and Collaltino as a warrior, can be found in Ann Rosalind Jones, *The Currency of Eros: Women's Love Lyric in Europe 1540-1620* (Bloomington: Indiana University Press, 1990): 119-21.

9. Justin Vitiello ("The Ambiguities of Martyrdom," *Modern Language Notes* 90 [1975]: 58-71), perceptively noticed that the scenario of the martyrdom of the poet dying for love in Stampa's poetry is similar, in many ways, to that of the mystic poets, Jacopone da Todi, St. Theresa of Jesus (of Avila), and St. John of the Cross. Vitiello successfully argued that Stampa, by virtue of her sacrifice for love, achieved moral superiority over her socially superior lover.

10. The *Accademie*, literary academies or intellectual coteries, were started by the humanists in Italy in the fifteenth century and flourished in the sixteenth and seventeenth centuries. These academies, with headquarters in different Italian towns, often took droll or funny names chosen with Socratic irony: *Gli Insensati* (Those without Wits), *I Rozzi* (The Uncouth Ones), *I Pazzi* (The Crazy Ones), *I Timidi* (The Shy Ones), etc. Upon receiving membership, members chose a fictional, often symbolic, name, that reflected their personalities and goals. For Stampa's entry into the *Accademia dei Dubbiosi* (the Doubtful Ones), she chose a name that was an ingenious metaphorical device by which she claimed ownership over the Collalto lands and vindicated what she must have perceived as her spurned rights.

For an interesting study of the underlying symbolic meaning of Stampa's pastoral poetry, written under the name of Anaxilla, see also Jones, *The Currency of Eros,* 118-54.

11. For a study of depression, melancholia, and mourning in Stampa's poetry, see Juliana Schiesari's *The Gendering of Melancholia* (Ithaca & London: Cornell University Press, 1992), 160-90. Schiesari sees Stampa as a poet attempting to do away with the historical limitations that deprived women of the potential to make viable claims in terms of loss and grief, and mourning "the deprivation that disallows women's voices from being accredited" (p. 169).

Translators' Note

The poems in this dual-language volume represent a selection from Gaspara Stampa's collected poems. There is no extant manuscript of Stampa's work. While she was alive, only three of her sonnets were published. They appeared in the anthology entitled, *Il sesto libro delle Rime di diversi eccellenti autori novamente raccolte e mandate in luce con un discorso di Girolamo Ruscelli* (Venice: G. M. Bonelli, 1553). The same three sonnets were later reprinted in the anthology, *Rime diverse d'alcune nobilissime e virtuossime donne raccolte per Messer Ludovico Domenichi* (Lucca: Busdrago, 1559).

Stampa's *Rime,* published by her sister Cassandra in October of 1554, represents one of the largest and most varied *canzonieri* in Italian literature, comprising 311 poems in all, which the poet had arranged in a chronological manner. A. Salza, the editor of the 1913 critical edition, made major changes to the structure of the original edition, reorganizing the material and dividing it into Love Poems and Occasional Poems. All modern editions, including ours, are based on Salza's critical edition – which restored the punctuation and the diacritical marks of the 1554 edition – and follow Salza's division of the material into two sections. The first, larger section, Love Poems *(Rime d'amore),* containing the love lyrics for Count Collaltino di Collalto, as well as the later love poems for Bartolomeo Zen, includes poems 1 to 245, all of which are sonnets, except for a *canzone,* two *sestinas,* nineteen madrigals, and five *capitoli* (tercets). The second, smaller section, Miscellaneous Poems *(Rime varie),* includes poems 246 to 311, all of which are sonnets, except for a *canzone,* a dialogue in quatrains, and two *capitoli.* It includes poems for friends and literati (such as Collaltino's brother, Vinciguerra, Domenico Venier, Speroni Speroni, Luigi Alamanni, Leonardo Emo, and others), a few occasional poems for Collaltino di Collalto, some poems for Stampa's women friends (Giovanna d'Aragona and Ippolita Mirtilla), some poems written on the occasion of the death of a nun (possibly Suor Angelica Paola de' Negri), and ends with several religious sonnets, in which Stampa – foreshadowing her untimely death – voices her weariness and confesses her repentance for a life too passionate, too free.

Very few of Stampa's poems have ever been translated into English. The translations in this volume represent the first rendition of a large corpus of Stampa's work in modern English. We have not attempted to present Stampa's collected poems in their entirety because of the size of the corpus, and, since several of the poems return to the same subjects, it was possible to make a broad, representative selection. In this volume, the number of each poem corresponds to the numbering in the Salza edition.

Since these poems are characteristic of the time in which they were written, the sixteenth century, in translating them we have tried to maintain a sense of the period, while at the same time avoiding archaic diction for the sake of the modern ear. Therefore, we have tried to strike a balance between modern English poetic diction and the Italian usage of Stampa's lifetime, since it did not feel right to us to present the poems in too strikingly a modern form. We have, however, changed and modernized the punctuation in the English versions, whenever it was necessary for the sake of clarity.

In translating these poems into English verse, we have kept as close as possible to the literal sense of the original text. For the sake of accuracy, we have not attempted to rhyme, except in very few cases: it is impossible to render the true sense of the Italian into English while trying to force a rhyming word at the end of each line, especially since English, compared with Italian, is very poor in rhymes. We did, however, feel very strongly that poetry in translation should be presented as verse, rather than prose, since the form of verse on the page raises different expectations in the reader than does prose.

The great majority of the poems in this volume are sonnets. As the reader no doubt knows, the Italian sonnet – a poetic form that originated in medieval Sicily and was later elaborated by the Tuscan *stil nuovo* poets –

is made of two quatrains (four-line stanzas) followed by two tercets (three-line stanzas). To translate the sonnets into English, we used the rather unsual form of the un-rhymed sonnet, preserving the line count and the structure of thought, while not straining for rhyme or even assonance. Since English verse depends on accent rather than syllable count, we have used iambic pentameter to represent the Italian hendecasyllable (eleven-syllable line). Thus some English lines have ten, and others eleven, syllables, as in Shakespeare or other poets using English blank verse (unrhymed iambic pentameter).

Included in this volume are eight of Stampa's madrigals (224, 229–33, 235 and 238) – short monostrophic songs, which originated in Italy in the fourteenth century. To translate them, we followed the Italian method of counting syllables, varying between seven- and eleven-syllable lines, as in the originals. In some of them we have used rhyme or near-rhyme, since these were after all musical forms, meant to be sung, and we felt it was necessary to give at least an approximation of the vowel sounds. However, it was not always possible to reconcile sound with sense, and here again we favored the latter. Poem 68 is a Petrarchan *canzone,* and we followed Stampa's structure, in which she used five thirteen-line stanzas and a three-line envoi. Poem 95 is a *sestina,* where the poetic form depends on the different positioning of repeated words rather than sounds. These are composed of six six-line stanzas with one three-line envoi where the end-words in the first stanza repeat in a

To My Illustrious Lord

Since my amorous pains, which for the love of Your Lordship I have written about in several letters and rhymes, have not been able, one by one, to make Your Lordship take pity on me, nor even to make you courteous enough to write me one word in return, I have resolved to collect them all in this book, to see if all together they will be able to do it. Here Your Lordship will not see the whole sea of my passions, my tears and my torments, because it is a bottomless sea; but only a little stream of them; nor should Your Lordship think that I have done this to make you aware of your cruelty, because one cannot talk of cruelty where there is no obligation, nor to constrain you; but rather to make you aware of your own greatness and to make you rejoice. Because, seeing that these fruits of love have issued from your harshness towards me, you can conjecture which ones will be produced by your pity, if it should ever happen that the heavens make you compassionate towards me: O noble object, O bright object, O divine object, since even in tormenting me you are beneficial and produce fruit. Read then, Your Lordship, when you have a rest from your dearest and greatest concerns, the notes of the grave and amorous cares of your most faithful and wretched Anaxilla; and from this reflection may you reckon how deeply she must feel in her soul; because certainly, if ever it will happen that my poor sad house be made worthy to receive Your Lordship, I am sure that the beds, the rooms, the halls and everything will tell of the laments, sobs, sighs and tears, which night and day I have shed, calling on Your Lordship's name, and nevertheless always blessing, in the midst of my greatest torments, the heavens and my good fortune for their cause; since it is far better to die for you, Count, than to rejoice for anyone else. But what am I doing? Since I am boring Your Lordship needlessly for too long, also insulting my poems, as if they could not express their motives, and as if they needed someone else's help? Trusting in them, then, I shall end, begging Your Lordship that, as last reward of my most faithful service, in receiving this poor booklet, you may give me the courtesy of even one sigh, which from afar may refresh the memory of his forgotten and abandoned Anaxilla. And you, little booklet of mine, trustee of my tears, present yourself in the most humble possible manner in front of my Lord, in the company of my candid faith; and if, when he receives you, you will see those fatal and eternal lights of mine (Collaltino's eyes) become even a little serene, may all of our labors be blessed and all of our hopes be happy; and so may you eternally remain with him in peace.

— Gaspara Stampa

Gaspara Stampa

Selected Poems

I ❦

Voi, ch'ascoltate in queste meste rime,
in questi mesti, in questi oscuri accenti
il suon degli amorosi miei lamenti
e de le pene mie tra l'altre prime,
    ove fia chi valor apprezzi e stime,
gloria, non che perdon, de' miei lamenti
spero trovar fra le ben nate genti,
poi che la lor cagione è sí sublime.
    E spero ancor che debba dir qualcuna:
– Felicissima lei, da che sostenne
per sí chiara cagion danno sí chiaro!
    Deh, perché tant'amor, tanta fortuna
per sí nobil signor a me non venne,
ch'anch'io n'andrei con tanta donna a paro?

I ᴥ

O you who listen to these mournful verses,
In these unhappy, in these somber accents,
To the sound of laments inspired by Love,
And of my pains, greater than any other,
I hope to find among some well-born people,   5
Wherever they may be, those who prize honor,
Not only pardon for my tears, but glory,
Because the reason for them is so lofty.
I dare to hope some woman will exclaim:
"Happy is she, she who has undergone   10
For such a noble cause, sorrow so noble!
Why were not such high fortune, such great love,
Granted to me, and such a splendid lord,
So I could walk as equal to that lady?"

2 ❧

Era vicino il dí che 'l Creatore,
che ne l'altezza sua potea restarsi,
in forma umana venne a dimostrarsi,
dal ventre virginal uscendo fore,
    quando degnò l'illustre mio signore,
per cui ho tanti poi lamenti sparsi,
potendo in luogo piú alto annidarsi,
farsi nido e ricetto del mio core.
    Ond'io sí rara e sí alta ventura
accolsi lieta; e duolmi sol che tardi
mi fe' degna di lei l'eterna cura.
    Da indi in qua pensieri e speme e sguardi
volsi a lui tutti, fuor d'ogni misura
chiaro e gentil, quanto 'l sol giri e guardi.

2 ❧

It was about the day when the Creator,
Who could have stayed in His sublime abode,
Came down to show Himself in human form,
Issuing from the Holy Virgin's womb,
When it occurred that my illustrious lord   5
For whom I wrote so many love laments,
Who could have found a nobler resting place,
Made his own nest and refuge in my heart.
So I embraced this rare and lofty fortune
With joy, only regretting that so late   10
I was made worthy by Eternal Care.
Since then I turned my hopes and thoughts and
    glances
On him alone, so noble, brave, and gentle,
Beyond all others that the sun beholds.

3 🦂

Se di rozzo pastor di gregge e folle
il giogo ascreo fe' diventar poeta
lui, che poi salse a sí lodata meta,
che quasi a tutti gli altri fama tolle,
    che meraviglia fia s'alza ed estolle
me bassa e vile a scriver tanta pièta,
quel che può piú che studio e che pianeta,
il mio verde, pregiato ed alto colle?
    La cui sacra, onorata e fatal ombra
dal mio cor, quasi súbita tempesta,
ogni ignoranza, ogni bassezza sgombra.
    Questa da basso luogo m'erge, e questa
mi rinova lo stil, la vena adombra;
tanta virtú nell'alma ognor mi desta!

3 ❧

If the Ascrean mountain made a poet
Of the rough shepherd with his flocks and herds,
Raising him up to such a peak of fame
As stole the praise from all the other writers,
What marvel is it if my high green hill   5
Much more than any planet or deep study
Has raised me, low and common as I am,
To write my story that will touch all hearts –
The hill whose sacred and resistless shade
Like a swift tempest, swept out of my heart   10
All ignorance and all baseness from my life.
This lifts me from my low position; this
Renews my style, whets my poetic vein,
And wakes the sleeping talent in my soul.

4 ❧

Quando fu prima il mio signor concetto,
tutti i pianeti in ciel, tutte le stelle
gli diêr le grazie, e queste doti e quelle,
perch'ei fosse tra noi solo perfetto.
Saturno diègli altezza d'intelletto;
Giove il cercar le cose degne e belle;
Marte appo lui fece ogn'altr'uomo imbelle;
Febo gli empí di stile e senno il petto;
Vener gli dié bellezza e leggiadria;
eloquenzia Mercurio; ma la luna
lo fe' gelato piú ch'io non vorria.
Di queste tante e rare grazie ognuna
m'infiammò de la chiara fiamma mia,
e per agghiacciar lui restò quell'una.

4 ≈

When my belovèd lord was first conceived,
All the stars in the sky and all the planets
Gave him their graces, and their varied gifts,
So he alone among us should be perfect.
Saturn gave him his height of intellect;   5
Jupiter, love for all that's fair and noble;
Mars made all men beside him seem unwarlike,
And Phoebus filled his heart with style and
    judgment.
Venus bestowed on him beauty and grace;
Mercury eloquence, but the pale Moon   10
Made his heart colder than my warm desire.
All of these stars, so lavish with their gifts,
Inflamed me with that shining torch of mine –
Only the Moon was left to freeze his heart.

5 ❧

Io assimiglio il mio signor al cielo
meco sovente. Il suo bel viso è 'l sole;
gli occhi, le stelle; e 'l suon de le parole
è l'armonia, che fa 'l signor di Delo.

Le tempeste, le piogge, i tuoni e 'l gelo
son i suoi sdegni, quando irar si suole;
le bonacce e 'l sereno è quando vuole
squarciar de l'ire sue benigno il velo.

La primavera e 'l germogliar de' fiori
è quando ei fa fiorir la mia speranza,
promettendo tenermi in questo stato.

L'orrido verno è poi, quando cangiato
minaccia di mutar pensieri e stanza,
spogliata me de' miei piú ricchi onori.

5 ⸙

Sometimes my mind will liken my belovèd
To everything in heaven; his fair face
Is like the sun; his eyes, the stars; his voice
The harmony made by the Lord of Delos.
Tempests and rain, the thunder and the lightning,   5
Are in his mien whenever he is angry;
His calms and cloudless days are when he wishes,
In kindness, to tear off the veil of wrath.
Springtime, the time when flowers bud and open,
Is when he makes my hope spring up anew   10
With promises to hold me in that state.
But dreadful winter comes, when of a sudden
He threatens change of both his mood and dwelling,
Despoiling me of all my dearest honors.

7

Chi vuol conoscer, donne, il mio signore,
miri un signor di vago e dolce aspetto,
giovane d'anni e vecchio d'intelletto,
imagin de la gloria e del valore:
    di pelo biondo, e di vivo colore,
di persona alta e spazioso petto,
e finalmente in ogni opra perfetto,
fuor ch'un poco (oimè lassa!) empio in amore.
    E chi vuol poi conoscer me, rimiri
una donna in effetti ed in sembiante
imagin de la morte e de' martíri,
    un albergo di fé salda e costante,
una, che, perché pianga, arda e sospiri,
non fa pietoso il suo crudel amante.

7 ❧

If, ladies, you desire to know my lord,
Look for a gentleman with sweet expression,
Though young in years, old in his intellect;
Image of valor and of warlike glory;
His hair is blond, and his complexion light,   5
He's tall in stature, with a manly chest,
Seeming perfection in his every act,
But, ah, in love not faithful to his word.
If you should care to know me, you might see,
A lady in her manner and appearance   10
Like Death herself and every kind of sorrow,
An inn of steady faith and constancy,
One who, for all her tears, her ardent sighs,
Can win no pity from her cruel lover.

8 ❧

Se, cosí come sono abietta e vile
donna, posso portar sí alto foco,
perché non debbo aver almeno un poco
di ritraggerlo al mondo e vena e stile?
S'Amor con novo, insolito focile,
ov'io non potea gir, m'alzò a tal loco,
perché non può non con usato gioco
far la pena e la penna in me simile?
E, se non può per forza di natura,
puollo almen per miracolo, che spesso
vince, trapassa e rompe ogni misura.
Come ciò sia non posso dir espresso;
io provo ben che per mia gran ventura
mi sento il cor di novo stile impresso.

8 ⁊

If I, who am an abject, low-born woman,
Can bear within me such lofty fire,
Why should I not possess at least a little
Poetic power to tell it to the world?
If Love, with such a new unheard-of flint   5
Lifted me up where I could never climb,
Why cannot I, in an unusual way,
Make pain and pen be equal in myself?
If Love cannot do this by force of nature,
Perhaps as by a miracle he may   10
Passing and bursting every common measure.
How that can be, I cannot well explain
But yet I feel, because of my great fortune,
My heart imprinted with a strong new style.

9 ❧

S'avien ch'un giorno Amor a me mi renda,
e mi ritolga a questo empio signore;
di che paventa, e non vorrebbe, il core,
tal gioia del penar suo par che prenda;
    voi chiamerete invan la mia stupenda
fede, e l'immenso e smisurato amore,
di vostra crudeltá, di vostro errore
tardi pentito, ove non è chi intenda.
    Ed io, cantando la mia libertade,
da cosí duri lacci e crudi sciolta,
passerò lieta a la futura etade.
    E, se giusto pregar in ciel s'ascolta,
vedrò forse anco in man di crudeltade
la vita vostra a mia vendetta involta.

9 ❧

If it should happen, one far day, that Love
Should give me back myself, setting me free,
From this harsh lord – I fear, rather than wish it,
Such joy, it seems, my heart takes from its pain –
You will in vain call on my unsurpassed   5
Fidelity and love, immense, unbounded,
Repenting of your cruelty and error
Too late, when you shall find no one to listen.
Then I, at last, singing my liberty,
Loosened from painful and restrictive ropes,   10
Shall go with living joy into my future.
And if in heaven rightful prayers are heard,
I shall at length behold your spirit bound
In hands of Cruelty, for my revenge.

12 ❧

Deh, perché cosí tardo gli occhi apersi
nel divin, non umano amato volto,
ond'io scorgo, mirando, impresso e scolto
un mar d'alti miracoli e diversi ?
Non avrei, lassa, gli occhi indarno aspersi
d' inutil pianto in questo viver stolto,
né l'alma avria, com'ha, poco né molto
di Fortuna o d'Amore onde dolersi.
E sarei forse di sí chiaro grido,
che, mercé de lo stil, ch'indi m' è dato,
risoneria fors'Adria oggi, e 'l suo lido.
Ond' io sol piango il mio tempo passato,
mirando altrove; e forse anche mi fido
di far in parte il foco mio lodato.

12 ⤦

Why did I wait so long to cast my eyes
Upon this godlike, superhuman face
Where I can see imprinted, like a sculpture,
A myriad of diverse and lofty wonders?
I would not then in vain have drowned my eyes   5
With useless weeping in my foolish life,
Nor would my soul feel very much or little,
Of Fortune or of Love to make me grieve.
I might already have achieved such fame
That, thanks to the high style inspired by him,   10
The Adriatic and its shores would ring.
It is for this I mourn my wasted time
In looking elsewhere; maybe I can still
At least in part make my great fire renowned.

13 🐾

Chi dará penne d'aquila o colomba
al mio stil basso, sí ch'ei prenda il volo
da l'Indo al Mauro e d'uno in altro polo,
ove arrivar non può saetta o fromba?
　　e, quasi chiara e risonante tromba,
la bellezza, il valor, al mondo solo,
di quel bel viso, ch' io sospiro e còlo,
descriva sí, che l'opra non soccomba?
　　Ma, poi che ciò m'è tolto, ed io poggiare
per me stessa non posso ove conviene,
sí che l'opra e lo stil vadan di pare,
　　l'udranno sol queste felici arene,
questo d'Adria beato e chiaro mare,
porto de' miei diletti e di mie pene.

13 ❧

Who will give wings of eagle or of dove
To my low style, to let it fly from India
To Mauretania, from South Pole to North,
Where never arrow or slingshot can reach?
And like a trumpet, resonant and clear,   5
May tell the matchless beauty and the valor
Of that fair face which I revere and sigh for,
So that the work itself will never die.
But since this gift was never given me
And by myself I can't climb high enough   10
To make the work and style of equal worth,
Only those happy sands will hear my song
Beside the clear, blest Adriatic sea,
Harbor of my delights and many pains.

17 ❦

Io non v'invidio punto, angeli santi,
le vostre tante glorie e tanti beni,
e que' disir di ciò che braman pieni,
stando voi sempre a l'alto Sire avanti;
  perché i diletti miei son tali e tanti,
che non posson capire in cor terreni,
mentr'ho davanti i lumi almi e sereni,
di cui conven che sempre scriva e canti.
  E come in ciel gran refrigerio e vita
dal volto Suo solete voi fruire,
tal io qua giú da la beltá infinita.
  In questo sol vincete il mio gioire,
che la vostra è eterna e stabilita,
e la mia gloria può tosto finire.

17 ❧

I do not envy you, O holy angels,
For your exalted glory and great blessing,
Nor the fulfillment of your ardent longings
Always to stand before the Face of God,
For my delights are such and so abundant   5
They cannot be contained in human heart,
While I enjoy the presence of those lights –
The eyes of him I ever praise in song.
And, as in heaven you enjoy refreshment
And life beneath the glory of His Face,   10
So I, below, in his supernal beauty.
In one sole point do you surpass my joy:
That yours is everlasting and unchanging,
But my delight and glory must soon end.

18 ❧

Quando i' veggio apparir il mio bel raggio,
parmi veder il sol, quand'esce fòra;
quando fa meco poi dolce dimora,
assembra il sol che faccia suo viaggio.
E tanta nel cor gioia e vigor aggio,
tanta ne mostro nel sembiante allora,
quanto l'erba, che pinge il sol ancora
a mezzo giorno nel piú vago maggio.
Quando poi parte il mio sol finalmente,
parmi l'altro veder, che scolorita
lasci la terra andando in occidente.
Ma l'altro torna, e rende luce e vita;
e del mio chiaro e lucido oriente
è 'l tornar dubbio e certa la partita.

18 ❧

Whenever I behold my lovely ray,
I think I see the sun on point of rising;
And when he deigns to stay with me awhile,
It seems the sun is crossing through the sky.
And then I feel such happiness and vigor   5
That I must show as much in my appearance
As does the grass, which the sun paints with color,
At noon time, in the fairest month of May.
But when at length my sun departs from me,
I see the sun of heaven when it darkens   10
And leaves the earth to sink down in the west.
But that sun will return with light and life,
While my sun's brilliant dawning and return
To me is doubtful; certain is the parting.

21 ❧

   — S'io, che son dio, ed ho meco tant'armi,
non posso star col tuo signor a prova,
ed è la sua bellezza unica e nova
pronta mai sempre a tante ingiurie farmi,
   come a tuo pro poss'ora io consigliarmi,
e darti il modo, con che tu rimova
quel saldo ghiaccio, che nel cor si trova,
per via di preghi, di consiglio o carmi?
   Ti bisogna aspettar tempo o fortuna,
che ti guidino a questo; ed altra via
non ti posso mostrar, se non quest'una. —
   Cosí mi dice, e poi si vola via;
ed io mi resto, al sole ed a la luna,
piangendo sempre la sventura mia.

21 🪓

"If I, who am a God, and so well-armed,
Can never win in contest with your lord
Whose beauty is unique and always new,
And ever ready to do me more harm,
How can I think of any way to help you   5
And give you any manner to remove
By way of prayers, or wisdom, or by songs,
The solid ice that lies inside his heart?
You must await propitious Time or Fortune
Till they show you the way, no other path   10
Can I point out to you, except this one."
Love says all this to me, then flies away,
And I am left, whether by sun or moon,
Forever weeping my unhappy fate.

22 ❦

Rivolgete talor pietoso gli occhi
da le vostre bellezze a le mie pene,
sí che quanta alterezza indi vi viene,
tanta quindi pietate il cor vi tocchi.
    Vedrete qual martír indi mi fiocchi,
vedrete vòte le faretre e piene,
che preste a' danni miei sempre Amor tiene,
quando avien che ver' me l'arco suo scocchi.
    E forse la pietá del mio tormento
vi moverá, dov'or ne gite altero,
non lo vedendo voi, qual io lo sento;
    cosí penosa io meno, e men voi fiero
ritornerete, e cento volte e cento
benedirete i ciel, che mi vi dièro.

22 ❧

Some time in pity turn your brilliant eyes
From your great beauty to my painful state,
So that as much as haughtiness is there,
Let so much pity for me touch my heart.
You'll see what bitter torment rains upon me,   5
You'll see Love's quiver empty and then filled
With darts he keeps ready to give me pain
Whenever he will bend his bow toward me.
And maybe pity for my pain will move you
Where now you walk about in scornful pride,   10
Since you don't see it deeply as I feel it.
Then I would be less sad and you less haughty
When you return. A hundred times and over
You'll bless the heavens that gave me to you.

24 ❧

Vengan quante fûr mai lingue ed ingegni,
quanti fûr stili in prosa, e quanti in versi,
e quanti in tempi e paesi diversi
spirti di riverenza e d'onor degni;
   non fia mai che descrivan l'ire e' sdegni,
le noie e i danni, che 'n amor soffersi,
perché nel vero tanti e tali fêrsi,
che passan tutti gli amorosi segni.
   E non fia anche alcun, che possa dire,
anzi adombrar la schiera de' diletti
ch'Amor, la sua mercé, mi fa sentire.
   Voi, ch'ad amar per grazia sète eletti,
non vi dolete dunque di patire;
perché i martir d'Amor son benedetti.

24 🦋

Let all the minds and tongues on earth come forth
With every style of prose as well as verse,
From every time and countries of all sorts:
Spirits to whom all reverence is due:
Not one could tell the anger and disdain,   5
Heartache and pain that Love has made me suffer,
Because they were so many and so great,
That they surpass all of Love's other sorrows.
And no one is there who can well describe
Or even sketch the number of delights   10
Which Love, in his good favor, made me feel.
You who are chosen by the grace of Love,
Do not repine, therefore, if you must suffer,
Since torments caused by love are always blest.

26 🥭

Arsi, piansi, cantai; piango, ardo e canto;
piangerò, arderò, canterò sempre
(fin che Morte o Fortuna o tempo stempre
a l'ingegno, occhi e cor, stil, foco e pianto)
   la bellezza, il valor e 'l senno a canto,
che 'n vaghe, sagge ed onorate tempre
Amor, natura e studio par che tempre
nel volto, petto e cor del lume santo;
   che, quando viene, e quando parte il sole,
la notte e 'l giorno ognor, la state e 'l verno,
tenebre e luce darmi e tôrmi suole,
   tanto con l'occhio fuor, con l'occhio interno,
agli atti suoi, ai modi, a le parole,
splendor, dolcezza e grazia ivi discerno.

26 ҉

I burnt, I wept, I sang – burn, weep and sing,
And I shall weep, burn, sing forever more
(Until Death, Time, or Fortune wash away
My talent, eyes, heart, style, my fire and tears)
The beauty, courage and deep intellect,   5
Which in a lovely, wise and honored manner,
Love, nature and the highest art have painted
Within the face, breast, heart of my true light
Who – when the sun itself rises or sets,
By night or day, in summer or in winter –   10
Gives me or takes away darkness or light.
Thus, with my outer or my inner eye,
I see in all his acts, manners and words
His splendor, and his sweetness and his grace.

27 ❧

Altri mai foco, stral, prigione o nodo
sí vivo e acuto, e sí aspra e sí stretto
non arse, impiagò, tenne e strinse il petto,
quanto 'l mi' ardente, acuto, acerba e sodo.
　Né qual io moro e nasco, e peno e godo,
mor' altra e nasce, e pena ed ha diletto,
per fermo e vario e bello e crudo aspetto,
che 'n voci e 'n carte spesso accuso e lodo.
　Né fûro ad altrui mai le gioie care,
quanto è a me, quando mi doglio e sfaccio,
mirando a le mie luci or fosche or chiare.
　Mi dorrá sol, se mi trarrá d'impaccio,
fin che potrò e viver ed amare,
lo stral e 'l foco e la prigione e 'l laccio.

27 ❧

Never did fire, darts, prison bars or chains
So lively, sharp, so harsh and so constraining
Consume or wound, confine and bind another
As do mine, burning, bitter, sharp and tight.
Nor as I die, am born, feel pain, rejoice,   5
Can any other woman feel as much,
For one firm, changing, fair and cruel face,
That I with voice or paper blame and praise.
Neither did any other hold so dear
The pain I feel when I undo myself   10
Gazing upon those eyes, now dark, now clear.
I'll only grieve while I can live and love,
If I should lose the burdens that I bear:
The fire, the darts, the prison, and the chains.

34 ❧

Sai tu, perché ti mise in mano, Amore,
gli stral tua madre, ed agli occhi la benda?
Perché quella saetti, impiaghi e fenda
i cor di questo e quel fido amatore;
  e con questi non possi veder fuore
de' colpi tuoi la crudeltá stupenda,
sí che pietoso affatto non ti renda,
o almen non tempri l'empio tuo furore.
  Che, se vedessi un dí la piaga mia,
o non saresti dio, ma cruda fèra,
o pietoso o men aspro ti faria.
  Non vorrei giá che tu vedessi in cera
i raggi del mio sol; ché ti parria
forse a l'incontro picciola e leggera.

34 ❧

Love, do you know why your fair mother gave you
These arrows to your hands, and bound your eyes?
That you may shoot the first wound and break
The heart of this or any faithful lover;
And tied the blindfold, so you cannot see   5
The dreadful cruelty you have inflicted
So that it will not let you suffer pity,
Or even moderate your impious furor.
For, if you saw one of my dreadful wounds,
You would not be a god, but a wild beast,   10
Or it might make you tender, or less fierce.
I would not wish you to come face to face
With the rays of my sun; my wound would seem,
Next to his greatness, small and even light.

41 ❧

Ahi, se cosí vi distrignesse il laccio,
come, misera, me strigne ed affrena,
non cerchereste d'una in altra pena
girmi traendo, e d'uno in altro impaccio;
    ma perch'io son di foco e voi di ghiaccio,
voi sète in libertade ed io 'n catena,
i' son di stanca e voi di franca lena,
voi vivete contento ed io mi sfaccio.
    Voi mi ponete leggi, ch'a portarle
non basterian le spalle di Milone,
non ch'io debile e fral possa osservarle.
    Seguite, poi che 'l ciel cosí dispone:
forse ch'un giorno Amor potria mutarle;
forse ch'un dí fará la mia ragione.

41 ❧

Oh, if the cord that binds me in my sorrow
And holds me back could only hold you too,
You would not try to pull me with your reins
From one misfortune to another one.
But since I am all fire and you all ice,   5
You live in freedom, but I live in chains;
Your breath flows easily, my own is labored;
You live contented, I destroy myself.
The laws you lay upon me are so heavy
That even Milo's shoulders could not bear them,   10
Much less can mine, so delicate and fragile.
But go your way, since heaven so decrees.
Perhaps the god of Love will change at last.
Perhaps this god some day will do me justice.

43 ❧

Dura è la stella mia, maggior durezza
è quella del mio conte: egli mi fugge,
i' seguo lui; altri per me si strugge,
i' non posso mirar altra bellezza.

Odio chi m'ama, ed amo chi mi sprezza;
verso chi m'è umíle il mio cor rugge,
e son umíl con chi mia speme adugge;
a cosí stranio cibo ho l'alma avezza.

Egli ognor dá cagione a novo sdegno,
essi mi cercan dar conforto e pace:
i' lasso questi, ed a quell'un m'attegno.

Cosí ne la tua scola, Amor, si face
sempre il contrario di quel ch'egli è degno:
l'umíl si sprezza, e l'empio si compiace.

43 ᴥ

Harsh is my fortune, but still harder fate
Is dealt me by my lord; he flees from me.
I follow him, while others pine for me,
But I cannot admire another's face.
I hate the one who loves, love him who scorns me.   5
Against the humble ones, my heart rebels,
But I am humble toward the one who spurns me.
So my soul starves for such a harmful food!
He gives me cause for anger every day,
The others try to give comfort and peace.   10
Those I deny, but cling to my tormentor.
Thus, in your school, O Love, the scholars win
The opposite of that which they deserve:
The humble are despised, the proud are praised.

45 ❧

Io vo pur descrivendo d'ora in ora
la beltá vostra e 'l vostro raro ingegno,
e 'l valor d'altro stil, che del mio, degno,
se non quant'ei piú d'altro mai v'onora:
    né, perch'io m'affatichi, giungo ancora
di tanti pregi vostri al minor segno,
conte, d'ogni virtú nido e sostegno,
senza cui la mia vita morte fôra.
    Cosí, s'io prendo a scriver, il mio foco
è tanto e tal, da ch'egli da voi nasce,
che, s'io ne dico assai, ne dico poco.
    Questo e quello il mio cor nutrisce e pasce,
e questo e quel mi dá martír e gioco:
cosí fui destinata entro le fasce.

45 ❧

I go on always, hour by hour, describing
Your beauty, your rare talent and your valor,
Worthy of genius loftier than mine,
And yet my pen praises you more than any.
Nor, much as I may toil at all my writing,   5
Do I ever strike the least point of my target,
O Count, nest and support of every good
Without whom all my life would be like death.
Thus, when I start to write of you, my fire
Is such, so ardent, since it comes from you,   10
That all I find to say is still too little.
But either way it nourishes my heart,
And either way brings suffering and joy.
To this end I was fated from my cradle.

47 ❧

Io son da l'aspettar omai sí stanca,
sí vinta dal dolor e dal disio,
per la sí poca fede e molto oblio
di chi del suo tornar, lassa, mi manca,
  che lei, che 'l mondo impalidisce e 'mbianca
con la sua falce e dá l'ultimo fio,
chiamo talor per refrigerio mio,
si 'l dolor nel mio petto si rinfranca.
  Ed ella si fa sorda al mio chiamare,
schernendo i miei pensier fallaci e folli,
come sta sordo anch'egli al suo tornare.
  Cosí col pianto, ond'ho gli occhi miei molli,
fo pietose quest'onde e questo mare;
ed ei si vive lieto ne' suoi colli.

47 ❧

I have become so weary of my waiting,
Defeated by the grieving and desire
Caused by the little faith and short remembrance
Of him for whose return I mourn in vain,
That I call her who makes the world turn pale   5
And with her scythe fulfills the final sentence,
Imploring her to bring me sweet relief
And free me from the sorrow of my heart.
She, though, deafens herself to my entreaties,
Repulsing all my weak and foolish thoughts,   10
Just as he shuts his ears against returning.
So, weeping till my eyelids overflow,
I pour my piteous tears into this sea,
While he lives happily among his hills.

49 ❧

Qual sempre a' miei disir contraria sorte
fra la spiga e la man mi s'è tramessa,
sí che la gioia, che mi fu promessa,
tarda tanto a venir per darmi morte?
    Le mie due vive, due fidate scorte,
il signor mio, anzi l'anima stessa,
l'imagin, che nel cor m'è sempre impressa,
perché non batte omai, lassa, a le porte?
    L'alma allargata a questa nova speme,
che ristretta nel duol prendea vigore,
mancherá tosto certo, se non viene.
    E saran de' miracoli d'Amore,
ch'un'ombra breve di sperato bene
tolga altrui vita, e dia vita il dolore.

49

What fate, always opposed to my desires,
Thrusts in between my hand and the ripe corn,
So that the joy that had been promised me
Arrives so late it only brings me death.
The two faithful companions of my heart,   5
The very soul of my beloved lord,
His image – which is printed in my heart –
Why do they never knock upon my door?
My soul, grown greater with this new-born hope,
Which, bound by grief, had started to lose vigor,   10
Will surely not survive unless he comes;
And it must be some miracle of Love
To make the shadow of a hoped-for good
Steal life away and give life to my sorrow.

55 ❧

Voi, che 'n marmi, in colori, in bronzo, in cera
imitate e vincete la natura,
formando questa e quell'altra figura,
che poi somigli a la sua forma vera,
    venite tutti in graziosa schiera
a formar la piú bella creatura,
che facesse giamai la prima cura,
poi che con le sue man fe' la primiera.
    Ritraggete il mio conte, e siavi a mente
qual è dentro ritrarlo, e qual è fore;
sí che a tanta opra non manchi niente.
    Fategli solamente doppio il core,
come vedrete ch'egli ha veramente
il suo e 'l mio, che gli ha donato Amore.

55 ·

You artists, who are able to reflect
In marble, bronze, and colors, or in wax,
A lifelike form precisely like the true one,
Even surpassing that which nature made,
Come all together in a gracious group   5
To shape the fairest creature the First Care
Ever produced, since in creation's time
With His own hands, he formed Adam and Eve.
Portray my count, and keep it well in mind
To show the inward man as well as outer,   10
That your portrayal may be lacking nothing.
Take special care to show his double heart –
As you well see he has just such a one:
His own and mine, given to him by Love.

56 ❦

Ritraggete poi me da l'altra parte,
come vedrete ch'io sono in effetto:
viva senz'alma e senza cor nel petto
per miracol d'Amor raro e nov'arte;
    quasi nave che vada senza sarte,
senza timon, senza vele e trinchetto,
mirando sempre al lume benedetto
de la sua tramontana, ovunque parte.
    Ed avertite che sia 'l mio sembiante
da la parte sinistra afflitto e mesto,
e da la destra allegro e trionfante:
    il mio stato felice vuol dir questo,
or che mi trovo il mio signor davante;
quello, il timor che sará d'altra presto.

56 ❧

Then paint my portrait from the other side,
Just as you see me, as I truly am,
Alive without a soul, breast without heart,
By an unheard-of miracle of Love.
And like a ship that moves without its rigging,   5
Lacking a rudder, lacking main- or foremast,
Gazing forever on that blest North Star
That guides the ship wherever it may go.
And then observe that on the left-hand side
My countenance is always sad and woeful,   10
But on the right is joyful and triumphant.
My happy side has only this one meaning:
That I am standing close beside my lord;
The sad, fear that another woman holds him.

64 ❧

Voi che novellamente, donne, entrate
in questo pien di téma e pien d'errore
largo e profondo pelago d'Amore,
ove giá tante navi son spezzate,

siate accorte, e tant'oltra non passate,
che non possiate infine uscirne fore,
né fidate in bonacce o 'n second'ôre;
ché come a me vi fian tosto cangiate.

Sia dal mio essempio il vostro legno scorto,
cui ria fortuna allor diede di piglio,
che piú sperai esser vicina al porto.

Sovra tutto vi do questo consiglio:
prendete amanti nobili; e conforto
questo vi fia in ogni aspro periglio.

64 &

You women who have newly entered in
To this great sea, so full of fear and error,
The large and fathomless ocean of love
Where many a ship before your own has sunk –
Be careful, do not venture any deeper   5
Than you can find a way of getting out.
Don't trust in favorable winds or tides
For they can change – just as they did for me.
And let your vessel learn from my example,
For mine was nearly wrecked by evil fortune   10
The moment I had hoped to reach my port.
And, above all, I give you this advice:
Take only noble lovers – this will be
A comfort to you in the gravest danger.

68 ❧

Chiaro e famoso mare,
sovra 'l cui nobil dosso
si posò 'l mio signor, mentre Amor volle;
rive onorate e care
(con sospir dir lo posso),
che 'l petto mio vedeste spesso molle;
soave lido e colle,
che con fiato amoroso
udisti le mie note,
d'ira e di sdegno vòte,
colme d'ogni diletto e di riposo;
udite tutti intenti
il suon or degli acerbi miei lamenti.
    I' dico che dal giorno
che fece dipartita
l'idolo, ond'avean pace i miei sospiri,
tolti mi fûr d'attorno
tutti i ben d'esta vita;
e restai preda eterna de' martìri:
e, perch'io pur m'adiri
e chiami Amor ingrato,
che m'involò sí tosto
il ben ch'or sta discosto,

68 ❦

Shining and famous sea
   Upon whose noble back
   My lord reposed as long as Love desired,
   Honored and lovely banks
   – I say it with a sigh –   5
   That often looked upon my tender heart,
   Sweet shore, belovèd hills
   That harkened to my notes
   Breathed forth in tones of love,
   Empty of wrath and scorn,   10
   But filled with all delight and gentle peace:
   Now hear with fixed attention
   The sound of my distressful, sad lamenting.
I say that from the day
   When he, my idol, left me,   15
   Who stilled my sighing with a perfect peace,
   The blessings of this life
   Were stolen from my side,
   And I was left eternal prey to sorrow.
   And therefore I am angry   20
   And I call Love ungrateful
   Who stole from me so soon
   That Good who keeps afar,

non per questo a pietade è mai tornato;
e tien l'usate tempre,
perch'io mi sfaccia e mi lamenti sempre.
   Deh fosse men lontano
almen chi move il pianto,
e chi move le giuste mie querele!
ché forse non invano
m'affligerei cotanto,
e chiamerei Amor empio e crudele,
ch'amaro assenzio e fele
dopo quel dolce cibo
mi fe', lassa, gustare
in tempre aspre ed amare.
O duro tòsco, che 'n amor delibo,
perché fai sí dogliosa
la vita mia, che fu giá sí gioiosa?
   Almen, poi che m'è lunge
il mio terrestre dio,
che sí lontano ancor m'apporta guai,
il duol che sí mi punge
non mandasse in oblio,
e l'udisse ei, per cui piansi e cantai:
men acerbi i miei lai,
men cruda la mia pena,
men fiero il mio tormento,
che giorno e notte sento,

And will not come to me for love or pity.
He goes his usual ways,   25
So that I grieve and pine, forever mournful.
If he were only near
   The cause of all my weeping,
   He who has moved me to my just complaints,
   Then maybe not in vain   30
   Would I afflict myself
   And call Love impious and fierce and cruel,
   Who made me taste so acrid
   A potion, gall and wormwood,
   After so sweet a feast!   35
   What must I feed on now,
   In these harsh, cruel days?
   You, bitter potion which I drink in love,
   Why do you make my life
   So sorrowful, that once was free and joyous?   40
At least, while he's far off,
   My own terrestrial god,
   Who even from such distance brings me pain,
   Why can't oblivion swallow
   The sorrow that so stabs me?   45
   Why can't he hear, for whom I wept and sang?
   My song would be less bitter,
   And less intense my pain,
   Less fierce would be the torment
   I suffer day and night.   50

fòra per la sua luce alma e serena;
e sariami 'l dispetto
dolce sovra ogni dolce alto diletto.

    S'egli è pur la mia stella,
e se s'accorda il cielo,
ch'io moia per cagion cosí gradita,
venga Morte, e con ella
Amor, e questo velo
tolgan, ed esca fuor l'alma smarrita;
che, da suo albergo uscita,
volerá lieta in parte,
dove s'avrá mercede
de la sua viva fede,
fede d'esser cantata in mille carte.
Ma, lassa, a che non torna
chi le tenebre mie con gli occhi adorna?

    Se tu fossi contenta,
canzon, come sei mesta,
n'andresti chiara in quella parte e 'n questa.

If I could see his loving, serene light,
Then even his disdain
Would turn to sweetness more than all delight.
If he is my own star
    And heaven will consent   55
    That I should perish for a cause so precious,
Then let Death come, and Love,
    That both may steal away
    My mortal veil, and let my lost soul flee,
Which, issuing from its inn,   60
    May fly to that high place
    Where mercy may be granted
Because of its live faith –
Faith that a thousand pages may yet sing...
Why will he not return,   65
    He who could lift my darkness with his eyes?

Envoi

If you could be content,
    My song, as you are sad,
    You would go brightly forth to all the world.

82 🦎

Qui, dove avien che 'l nostro mar ristagne,
conte, la vostra misera Anassilla,
quando la luna agghiaccia e 'l sol favilla,
pur voi chiamando, si lamenta ed agne.
Voi, dove avien che l'Oceano bagne,
la notte, il giorno, a l'alba ed a la squilla,
menando vita libera e tranquilla,
mirate lieto il mar e le campagne.
E sí l'assenzia e 'l poco amor v'invola
la memoria di lei, la vostra fede,
che pur non le scrivete una parola.
O fra tutt'altre mia miseria sola!
o pena mia, ch'ogn'altra pena eccede!
Ciò si comporta, Amor, ne la tua scola?

82 ও

Here, where our sea becomes a calm lagoon,
Count, your unhappy Anaxilla grieves,
Whether the moonlight chills or sunshine burns,
Calling for you, while she laments and weeps,
You who are where the ocean bathes the shore,   5
By night or day, by dawning or by sunset,
Living a life of freedom and of calm,
Happily gazing at the sea and landscape,
And so your absence and the little love,
Destroy the memory of her, your vows,   10
So that you fail to write a little word.
My misery's unique among all others.
This grief of mine exceeds all other griefs.
Is this the teaching in your school, O Love?

87

Prendi, Amor, i tuoi strali e la tua face,
ch'io ti rinunzio i torti e le fatiche,
le voglie a' propri danni sempre amiche,
la guerra certa e la dubbiosa pace.
   Trova un novo soggetto e piú capace,
cui 'l tuo foco arda e la tua rete intriche,
ch'io per me non vo' piú che mi si diche:
– Questa per altri indarno arde e si sface. –
   Io son dal grave essilio tuo tornata,
e son resa a me stessa, e non men pento,
mercé di lui che m'ha la via mostrata.
   E ne' miei danni ho pur questo contento,
ch'almen, s'io fui da te sí mal trattata,
alta fu la cagion del mio tormento.

87 ⁊

Love, take away your arrows and your torch
For I renounce your labors and your wrongs,
Your wishes always tending to my harm,
Inevitable wars, uncertain peace.
Go seek another and a stronger subject   5
To kindle with your flame, snare in your nets.
I do not want it ever said of me:
"This lady burns and kills herself in vain."
I have returned now from my painful exile,
Restored to my true self, and do not grieve,   10
Thanks to the one who shows me the right way.
Now in my pain I have this consolation:
Although I was abused by you so harshly,
Most noble was the source of all my sorrows.

88 ⁊

Lassa, chi turba la mia lunga pace?
chi rompe il sonno e l'alta mia quiete?
chi mi stilla nel cor novella sete
di gir seguendo quel che piú mi sface?
  Tu, Amore, il cui strale e la cui face
ogni contento uman recide e miete,
tu ber mi desti del tuo fiume Lete,
che piú mi nòce, quanto piú mi piace.
  Ahi, quando fia giamai ch'un giorno possa
voler col mio voler, resa a me stessa,
del grave giogo periglioso scossa?
  Quando fia mai che la sembianza impressa
dentro a le mie midolle e dentro a l'ossa
mi smaghi Amor, e' miei martír con essa?

88 ≷

Who is it who disturbs my long-held peace?
Who breaks my sleep and my exalted calm?
Who pours into my heart another thirst
To follow ever that which most destroys me?
You, Love, whose arrows and whose flaming torch   5
Wound and cut down all human happiness!
You made me drink of your dark river Lethe
Which pleases me the more, the more it harms me.
When may it happen, on some future day,
That I may freely will, my will restored,   10
Unshackled from the burden of your yoke?
When will it happen that Love will excise
That image stamped within my very marrow,
And, doing so, will kill my pain as well?

91 ❧

Novo e raro miracol di natura,
ma non novo né raro a quel signore,
che 'l mondo tutto va chiamando Amore,
che 'l tutto adopra fuor d'ogni misura:
    il valor, che degli altri il pregio fura,
del mio signor, che vince ogni valore,
è vinto, lassa, sol dal mio dolore,
dolor, a petto a cui null'altro dura.
    Quant'ei tutt'altri cavalieri eccede
in esser bello, nobile ed ardito,
tanto è vinto da me, da la mia fede.
    Miracol fuor d'amor mai non udito!
Dolor, che chi nol prova non lo crede!
Lassa, ch'io sola vinco l'infinito!

91 ❧

A rare, unheard-of miracle of nature,
But neither rare nor foreign to that Lord
Whom all the world calls by the name of Love,
Who, beyond any measure, conquers all.
The valor of my lord, who steals the honors   5
From every other gentleman of valor
Is conquered by the sorrow of my heart –
A sorrow that outlasts all other griefs.
As much as he excels all other knights
In handsome form, nobility, and courage,   10
He is surpassed by my undying faith –
A miracle unheard-of save in love,
A grief no one believes who has not felt it –
Thus, I alone defeat infinity!

92 ❧

Quasi quercia di monte urtata e scossa
da ogni lato e da contrari venti,
che, sendo or questi or quelli piú possenti,
per cader mille volte e mille è mossa,
   la vita mia, questa mia frale possa,
combattuta or da speme or da tormenti,
non sa, lontani i chiari lumi ardenti,
in qual parte piegar omai si possa.
   Or m'affidan le carte del mio bene,
or mi disperan poi l'altrui parole;
ei mi dice: — Io pur vengo; — altri: — Non viene. —
   Sia morte meco almen, piú che non suole,
pietosa a trarmi fuor di tante pene,
se non debbo veder tosto il mio sole.

92 🦋

As when a mountain oak, struck and beaten
From every side by fierce, contrary winds
(One being stronger now, and then the other),
Thousands of times seems on the point of falling,
Just so my life, my weak and fragile powers   5
– Beaten by hope at times, at times by fear,
When my two shining lights are far away –
Can't tell which is the better way to lean.
Sometimes my lover's letters reassure me,
Then other people's words make me despair.   10
He says, "I come," the others, "He's not coming."
May Death, more than her wont, take pity on me
And kindly lift me out of such great pain,
Unless I see my sun before too long.

95 ❧

Menami, Amor, omai, lassa! il mio sole,
che mi solea non pur far chiaro il giorno,
ma non men che 'l dì chiara anco la notte,
tal ch' io sprezzava il ritornar de l'alba,
sí di quest'occhi la sua vaga luce
disgombrava le tenebre e la nebbia.

Ed ora piú non veggio altro che nebbia,
poi che l'usato mio lucente sole,
con la sua e del mondo altera luce
lume facendo in altra parte e giorno,
vuol che mai non si rompa per me l'alba,
perché da me non fugga unqua la notte.

Deh discacciasse il vel di questa notte,
il vel di tanta e sí importuna nebbia,
e a l'apparir del suo ritorno l'alba
mi rimenasse il mio bramato sole,
sí che lieta vedessi ancora un giorno,
pria che chiudessi in tutto esta mia luce!

95 ❧

Lead me, O Love, for I have lost my sun
That used not only to make bright my day
But even brought new daylight into night
So I could well disprize the coming dawn
When from his eyes the lovely streams of light   5
Would drive away the shadows and the mist.

Now I see nothing but this heavy mist,
Because my dearly loved, once constant sun
Who brought me – and the world – his lofty light,
Takes to another hemisphere his day   10
And wills for me never to see the dawn
But dwell forever in this bitter night.

Alas, who can relieve me of this night
And tear away this blinding veil of mist
By causing his return, bringing the dawn;   15
Who will restore to me my longed-for sun,
So that with gladness I may greet the day
Before I leave forever this world's light?

Ben fôra chiara e graziosa luce,
che procedesse a sí beata notte;
ben fôra chiaro e desiato giorno,
e disgombrato di tempeste e nebbia,
che mostrasse a quest'occhi il lor bel sole,
spuntando tra le rose e tra i fior l'alba.

Pur ch'innanzi che 'l ciel mi renda l'alba,
morte amara non spenga la mia luce,
invidiando a lei l'amato sole;
e, chiusi gli occhi in sempiterna notte,
ne vada, lassa, a star fra quella nebbia,
dove mai non si vede il chiaro giorno.

Tu dunque, Amor, che fai di notte giorno,
e puoi condurmi in un momento l'alba,
e via cacciar de' miei martír la nebbia,
e di tenebre oscure trar la luce,
rompi omai 'l vel di questa lunga notte,
et adduci a quest'occhi il mio bel sole.

Vivo sol, che solei far chiaro il giorno,
mentre la luce mia non vide nebbia,
perché non meni a la mia notte l'alba?

Indeed, it would be clear and gracious light
That would precede for me such blessèd night,   20
Bringing anew a joyous shining day
Cleared of all storms and every heavy mist,
And showing to my eyes their well-loved sun
Opening flowers and roses in new dawn.

Before the heavens shall restore my dawn,   25
O let not bitter Death put out my light,
Envying my enjoyment of my sun,
When, with my eyes closed in eternal night,
I leave, alas, to dwell in heavy mist
Where one may never hope to see bright day.   30

You, therefore, Love, who turn dark night to day
And can conduct me momently to dawn,
Drive from my suffering heart this choking mist
And out of deepest shadows bring new light –
Break for me now the veil of this long night   35
And bring before my eyes my lovely sun!

O living sun, who used to light the day
When I saw light and never dwelt in mist,
Can you not bring to my dark night new dawn?

97 ❧

O gran valor d'un cavalier cortese,
d'aver portato fin in Francia il core
d'una giovane incauta, ch'Amore
a lo splendor de' suoi begli occhi prese!
    Almen m'aveste le promesse attese
di temprar con due versi il mio dolore,
mentre, signor, a procacciarvi onore
tutte le voglie avete ad una intese.
    I' ho pur letto ne l'antiche carte
che non ebber a sdegno i grandi eroi
parimente seguir Venere e Marte.
    E del re, che seguite, udito ho poi
che queste cure altamente comparte,
ond' è chiar dagli espèri ai lidi eoi.

97 ❧

O mighty valor of a courteous knight
Who carried off to France a loving heart
Of one incautious woman, one whom Love
Took captive through the splendor of your eyes!
At least you kept one promise made to me –   5
To temper my sharp pain with two sweet verses,
While you, my lord, in your pursuit of honor
Direct all your desires to that goal.
Yet have I read, written in ancient pages,
That the great heroes of those olden days   10
Could equally adore Venus and Mars;
And I have heard it said, the king you follow
Can nobly serve both these divinities –
So that his fame resounds from West to East.

98 ◌

Conte, il vostro valor ben è infinito,
sí che vince qualunque alto valore,
ma verissimamente è via minore
del duol, ch'amando io ho per voi patito.
    E, se non s'è fin qui letto et udito
de l'infinito cosa unqua maggiore,
questi sono i miracoli d'Amore,
che vince ciò che 'n cielo è stabilito.
    Tempo giá fu, che l'alta gioia mia
di gran lunga avanzava anco il mio duolo,
mentre dolce la speme entro fioria:
    or ella è gita, ed ei rimaso è solo,
dal dí che per mia stella acerba e ria
prendeste, ahi lassa! verso Francia il volo.

98 ?

My Count, your valor is so infinite
That it defeats the valor of all others,
But truly it's inferior to the pain
That I have suffered through my love for you.
Though nothing ever yet was read or heard   5
That could be greater than the infinite,
The miracles of Love are so immense
That they can vanquish the decrees of heaven.
There was a time when my deep joy in you
Could overcome by far the grief I felt,   10
For Hope still blossomed sweetly in my heart.
Now hope is gone and grief remains alone,
Since, owing to my bitter, evil star,
You, my dear lord, took flight from me to France.

100 ❦

O beata e dolcissima novella,
o caro annunzio, che mi promettete
che tosto rivedrò le care e liete
luci e la faccia graziosa e bella;
    o mia ventura, o mia propizia stella,
ch'a tanto ben serbata ancor m'avete,
o fede, o speme, ch'a me sempre sète
state compagne in dura, aspra procella;
    o cangiato in un punto viver mio
di mesto in lieto; o queto, almo e sereno
fatto or di verno tenebroso e rio;
    quando potrò giamai lodarvi a pieno?
come dir qual nel cor aggio disio?
di che letizia io l'abbia ingombro e pieno?

100 🦗

O blissful, dear, and sweetest of all news,
Message of joy, in which you promise me
That soon I'll see again the dear and happy
Lights, and that face so beautiful and gracious.
O my good fortune, my propitious star,   5
That has preserved me for so good an end,
O faith, O hope, you who have been to me
My true companions through the bitter storm!
O life of mine, changed in a single moment
From grief to joy, to quiet, rest and calm   10
Out of the winter that was dark and evil!
When can I give you your full due of praise,
And say what great desire is in my heart,
So full of joy, almost to overflowing?

101 ᶠ

Con quai degne accoglienze o quai parole
raccorrò io il mio gradito amante,
che torna a me con tante glorie e tante,
quante in un sol non vide forse il sole?
    Qual color or di rose, or di viole
fia 'l mio? qual cor or saldo ed or tremante,
condotta innanzi a quel divin sembiante,
ch'ardir e téma insieme dar mi suole?
    Osarò io con queste fide braccia
cingerli il caro collo, ed accostare
la mia tremante a la sua viva faccia?
    Lassa, che pur a tanto ben penare
temo che 'l cor di gioia non si sfaccia:
chi l'ha provato se lo può pensare.

101 𝕖

With what sufficient greetings or what words
Shall I receive my dearly cherished lover
Who now returns to me with such great glories
As the sun never saw in one sole man?
What color – rosy-red or violet-pale –   5
Will mine be, as my heart is brave or fearful
When I am led before his noble form
Which makes me bold and timid all at once?
And will I dare embrace with faithful arms
His lovely neck, or lift my trembling face   10
To press against his glowing, vivid cheek?
While I am suffering such a painful good,
I fear my heart will break with too much joy:
Only she who has felt it understands.

102 🦋

Via da me le tenebre e la nebbia,
che mi son sempre state agli occhi intorno
sei lune e piú, che 'n Francia fe' soggiorno
lui, che 'l mio cor, come gli piace, trebbia.
    È ben ragion ch'asserenarmi io debbia,
or che 'l mio sol m'ha rimenato il giorno;
or c'han pace le guerre, che d'attorno,
mi fûr, qual vide Trasimeno e Trebbia.
    Sia ogni cosa in me di riso piena,
poi che seco una schiera di diletti
a star meco il mio sol almo rimena.
    Sia la mia vita in mille dolci, eletti
piaceri involta, e tutta alma e serena,
e se stessa gioendo ognor diletti.

102 ❧

Away from me, you shadows and dark mists
Which have been constantly before my eyes
Six months and more, since he went off to France,
He who torments my heart as he desires.
Now it is time to be serene again,   5
Now that my sun has ushered back the day,
Now that the wars have ceased to rage around him –
Battles like Trebbia and Trasimene.
May everything in me be filled with laughter
Now that my sun returns to stay with me,   10
Bringing with him a swarm of choice delights,
Now may my soul be wrapt in countless pleasures,
A thousand sweets, and all my life serene,
Rejoicing in itself with sheer contentment.

104 &

O notte, a me più chiara e più beata
che i più beati giorni ed i più chiari,
notte degna da' primi e da' più rari
ingegni esser, non pur da me, lodata;
    tu de le gioie mie sola sei stata
fida ministra; tu tutti gli amari
de la mia vita hai fatto dolci e cari,
resomi in braccio lui che m' ha legata.
    Sol mi mancò che non divenni allora
la fortunata Alcmena, a cui sté tanto
più de l'usato a ritornar l'aurora.
    Pur così bene io non potrò mai tanto
dir di te, notte candida, ch'ancora
da la materia non sia vinto il canto.

104 ⁊

O night, more glorious and more blest to me
Than are the brightest and most blissful days!
Night, worthy to be praised by the most brilliant
Of human minds, not only by my words.
You only were the faithful minister   5
Of all my joys; and all the bitterness
That had oppressed me you made sweet and dear,
Bringing back to my arms him who had bound me.
I only lacked the gift that was bestowed
On fortunate Alcmena, when you lingered   10
Far past the usual hour of dawn's return.
And yet I cannot say so much of you,
O shining night, but that this song of mine
Will not be overwhelmed by what it sings.

106 ❧

O diletti d'amor dubbi e fugaci,
o speranza che s'alza e cade spesso,
e nasce e more in un momento istesso:
o poca fede, o poco lunghe paci!
  Quegli, a cui dissi: – Tu solo mi piaci, –
è pur tornato, io l'ho pur sempre presso,
io pur mi specchio e mi compiaccio in esso,
e ne' begli occhi suoi chiari e vivaci;
  e tuttavia nel cor mi rode un verme
di fredda gelosia, freddo timore
di tosto tosto senza lui vederme.
  Rendi tu vana la mia téma, Amore,
tu, che beata e lieta pòi tenerme,
conservandomi fido il mio signore.

106 &

Pleasures of love, so doubtful and so fleeting,
O hope, which soars and then so often falls,
Is born, then dies within the selfsame moment!
O little faith, O peaceful times too short!
The one to whom I said, "You alone please me"   5
Has now returned, I have him near me always;
In him I'm mirrored, only pleased in him
And in his beautiful, vivacious eyes.
Yet all the time a worm gnaws at my heart,
Of icy jealousy and chilling fear   10
That soon, soon, I shall find myself without him.
O Love, destroy this foolish fear of mine,
You who can make me blissful and serene,
Keeping my lord forever true to me.

110 ⁊

Chi può contar il mio felice stato,
l'alta mia gioia e gli alti miei diletti?
O un di que' del ciel angeli eletti,
o altro amante, che l'abbia provato.
  Io mi sto sempre al mio signor a lato,
godo il lampo degli occhi e 'l suon dei detti,
vivomi de' divini alti concetti,
ch'escon da tanto ingegno e sí pregiato.
  Io mi miro sovente il suo bel viso,
e mirando mi par veder insieme
tutta la gloria e 'l ben del paradiso.
  Quel che sol turba in parte la mia speme,
è 'l timor che da me non sia diviso;
ché 'l vorrei meco fin a l'ore estreme.

110 ❧

Who can describe how happy is my state,
Exalted joy and all my rare delights?
Either an angel in the courts of heaven,
Or any lover who has felt the same.
Now I live always with my lord beside me,   5
Revel in his bright eyes, his lovely speech;
I feed upon his high and godlike thoughts
Issuing from his noble, lofty mind.
I often gaze upon his handsome face
And as I look I seem to see combined   10
The glory and the joy of paradise.
The only thing that can perturb my hope
Is fear that he must part from me some day:
I want him near me till my final hour.

III 🕿

Pommi ove 'l mar irato geme e frange,
ov'ha l'acqua piú queta e piú tranquilla;
pommi ove 'l sol piú arde e piú sfavilla,
o dove il ghiaccio altrui trafige ed ange;
 pommi al Tanai gelato, al freddo Gange,
ove dolce rugiada e manna stilla,
ove per l'aria empio velen scintilla,
o dove per amor si ride e piange;
 pommi ove 'l crudo Scita ed empio fere,
o dove è queta gente e riposata,
o dove tosto o tardi uom vive e père:
 vivrò qual vissi, e sarò qual son stata,
pur che le fide mie due stelle vere
non rivolgan da me la luce usata.

III ﷼

Place me where ocean breaks with angry roar,
Or where the waters lie serene and calm,
Place me wherever sun shoots sparks that scorch
Or where the ice pierces with sharpest pain,
Place me beside the frozen Don, by Ganges   5
Where the sweet dew and manna are distilled,
Or where the bitter air sparkles with poison,
Wherever people laugh and cry for love.
Place me where cruel, heartless Scythians strike,
Or where the people live in peace and quiet,   10
Or where one lives and dies, too soon, too late –
I shall live as I've lived, be what I've been,
As long as my two faithful stars still shine
And will not turn their light away from me.

114 ❧

Mille volte, signor, movo la penna
per mostrar fuor, qual chiudo entro il pensiero,
il valor vostro e 'l bel sembiante altero,
ove Amor e la gloria l'ale impenna;
    ma perché chi cantò Sorga e Gebenna,
e seco il gran Virgilio e 'l grande Omero
non basteriano a raccontarne il vero,
ragion ch'io taccia a la memoria accenna.
    Però mi volgo a scriver solamente
l'istoria de le mie gioiose pene,
che mi fan singolar fra l'altra gente:
    e come Amor ne' be' vostr'occhi tiene
il seggio suo, e come indi sovente
sí dolce l'alma a tormentar mi viene.

114 ᵇ

A thousand times, my lord, I move my pen
To show what I keep hidden in my heart:
Your valor, and your handsome, proud appearance
Where Love and Glory spread their wings for flight.
But since he who sang Sorga and Gebenna   5
Along with Virgil and all-famous Homer
Would not be able to express the truth,
My reason tells me I should keep my silence.
Therefore I set myself only to write
The truthful story of my joyful pains   10
That make me singular among all people,
And tell how Love keeps in your brilliant eyes
His throne, and often comes from there to bring
So sweetly joy and anguish to my soul.

117 ❧

A che vergar, signor, carte ed inchiostro
in lodar me, se non ho cosa degna,
onde tant'alto onor mi si convegna;
e, se ho pur niente, è tutto vostro?
   Entro i begli occhi, entro l'avorio e l'ostro,
ove Amor tien sua gloriosa insegna,
ove per me trionfa e per voi regna,
quanto scrivo e ragiono mi fu mostro.
   Perché ciò che s'onora e 'n me si prezza,
anzi s'io vivo e spiro, è vostro il vanto,
a voi convien, non a la mia bassezza.
   Ma voi cercate con sí dolce canto,
lassa, oltra quel che fa vostra bellezza,
d'accrescermi piú foco e maggior pianto.

117 🦋

Why do you waste, my lord, paper and ink
In praising me, since I have nothing worthy
Of such high honor as you pay to me,
Or, if I have, it is all due to you?
From two fine eyes, from ivory and crimson,   5
Where Love displays his glorious escutcheon,
Triumphing over me, reigning through you,
I have learned everything I write and think.
So all you honor, all you praise in me,
Even my life and death, is all your merit –   10
To be ascribed to you, not to my lowness.
But now, alas, you seek in lovely song,
Beyond what you accomplish with your beauty,
To add fire to my flame, to cause more tears.

125 ❧

—Vorrei che mi dicessi un poco, Amore,
c'ho da far io con queste tue sorelle
Temenza e Gelosia? ed ond'è ch'elle
non sanno star se non dentro il mio core?
    Tu hai mille altre donne, che l'ardore
provan, com'io, de l'empie tue facelle:
or manda dunque queste a star con quelle,
fa' ch'un dí n'escan dal mio petto fore.
    — Io ho ben – mi dic'ei – mille persone
a chi mandarle; ma nessuna d'esse
ha, qual tu, da temer alta cagione.
    Le luci ch'ami son le luci stesse,
che, per dar gelosia e passione
a tutto il mondo, la mia madre elesse.

125 ❧

I wish that you could tell me, Love, a little,
What I should do with Fear and Jealousy,
Your cruel sisters. For what reason they
Do not know where to live but in my heart?
You have a thousand other ladies who   5
Can feel, as I, the burning of your darts:
Go send your sisters off to live with them,
And make them go away from my sore heart.
"I have," says he, "a thousand other people
To send them to, but not a one of those   10
Has such a noble cause for fearing them.
The lights you love, they are the very lights
My Mother Venus chose to give the world
Passion and Jealousy in every part."

126 ❧

Cosí m'acqueto di temer contenta,
e di viver d'amara gelosia,
pur che l'amato lume lo consenta,
pur che non spiaccia a lui la pena mia.
    Perch'è piú dolce se per lui si stenta,
che gioir per ogn'altro non saria;
ed io per me non fia mai che mi penta
di sí gradita e nobil prigionia;
    perché capir un'alma tanto bene,
senza provarvi qualche cosa aversa,
questa terrena vita non sostiene.
    Ed io, che sono in tante pene immersa,
quando avanti il suo raggio almo mi viene,
resto da quel ch'esser solea diversa.

126 ⅋

So I must calm myself, content with fearing
And living on in bitter jealousy
As long as my belovèd light consents,
As long as my distress does not displease him,
Since suffering on his account is sweeter   5
Than joy with any other man would be.
So, for myself, I never shall repent
Of such a sweet, of such a noble prison,
Because our earthly life will not allow us
So wholly to accept another soul   10
As not to feel in it something adverse.
And I, who am immersed in so much grief,
When his bright ray appears in front of me
Am glad to change from what I used to be.

129 ❦

O mia sventura, o mio perverso fato,
o sentenzia nemica del mio bene,
poi che senza mia colpa mi conviene
portar la pena de l'altrui peccato.
    Quando si vide mai reo condannato
a la morte, a l'essilio, a le catene
per l'altrui fallo e, per maggior sue pene,
senza esser dal suo giudice ascoltato?
    Io griderò, signor, tanto e sí forte,
che, se non li vorrete ascoltar voi,
udranno i gridi miei Amore o Morte;
    e forse alcun pietoso dirá poi:
– Questa locò per sua contraria sorte
in troppo crudo luogo i pensier suoi.

129 ❧

O my misfortune, O my perverse fate,
O judgment, enemy of all my good,
Since I must suffer, through no fault of mine
The penalty due to another's sin!
Where did one ever see a man condemned   5
To death, to exile, or imprisonment
For someone else's crime, and even worse,
Without a hearing given by his judge?
So I shall call aloud, my lord, so strongly,
That if you will not listen to my cries,   10
Both Love and Death will hear my anguished voice.
Maybe some sympathetic soul will say,
"Urged by contrary fate, this woman lodged
Her thoughts and feelings in too hard a place."

132 ❦

Quando io dimando nel mio pianto Amore,
che cosí male il mio parlar ascolta,
mille fiate il dí, non una volta,
ché mi fere e trafigge a tutte l'ore:
— Come esser può, s'io diedi l'alma e 'l core
al mio signor dal dí ch'a me l'ho tolta,
e se ogni cosa dentro a lui raccolta
è riso e gioia, è scema di dolore,
ch'io senta gelosia fredda e temenza,
e d'allegrezza e gioia resti priva,
s'io vivo in lui, e in me di me son senza ?
— Vo' che tu mora al bene ed al mal viva —
mi risponde egli in ultima sentenza; —
questo ti basti, e questo fa' che scriva.

132 ?

When in my weeping I inquire of Love
(Who so unwillingly gives ear to me)
A thousand times a day – never just once –
Why he will wound and pierce me all the time:
"How can it be, since I gave heart and soul   5
To him, the day I took them both from me,
If everything enclosed within his breast
Is only joy and laughter, never sorrow,
How can I feel cold jealousy and fear
And be deprived of all my joyfulness,   10
Living in him, and never in myself?"
"I bid you die to joy and live in grief,"
Love answers me in his hard final sentence.
"Let this suffice you, that it makes you write."

133 ð

Così, senza aver vita, vivo in pene,
e, vivendo ov'è gioia, non son lieta;
così fra viva e morta Amor mi tiene,
e vita e morte ad un tempo mi vieta.
    Tal la sua sorte a ognun nascendo viene,
tal fu il mio aspro e mio crudo pianeta;
di sí rio frutto in sitibonde arene,
senza mai sparger seme, avien ch'io mieta.
    E s'io voglio per me stessa finire
con la vita i tormenti, non m'è dato,
ché senza vita un uom non può colpire.
    Qual fine Amore e 'l ciel m'abbia serbato
io non so, lassa, e non posso ridire;
so ben ch'io sono in un misero stato.

133 𝓔

Thus, without having life, I live in pain,
And, living where is joy, I am not glad;
So Love maintains me between life and death,
And life and death alike withholds from me.
As each one's fate is given out at birth,   5
And my birth planet was so harsh and cruel
That I must reap out of these thirsty sands
This evil fruit which I have never sown.
And if I wish to finish my own life,
And with my life my pain, I'm not allowed,   10
For without life one has no power to act.
What end Love and the heavens hold for me
I do not know, and so I cannot say.
I know well that I am in wretched state.

135 ✤

Quanto è questo fatto ora aspro e selvaggio
di dolce, ch'esser suole, e lieto mare!
Dopo il vostro da noi allontanare
quanta compassion a me propria aggio,
    tanto ho invidia al bel colle, al pino, al faggio,
che gli fanno ombra, al fiume, che bagnare
gli suole il piede ed a me nome dare,
che godono or del vostro vivo raggio.
    E, se non che egli è pur quell'il bel nido,
dove nasceste, io pregherei che fesse
il ciel lui ermo, lor secchi e quel torbo:
    per questo io resto, e prego voi, o fido
del mio cor speglio, ove mi tergo e forbo,
a tornar tosto e serbar le promesse.

135 ❧

How harsh and savage has this place become,
This lovely sea that used to be so sweet!
After you moved so far away from me,
I feel as much compassion for myself
As I feel envy toward the lovely hill,   5
The pines, the beeches that provide your shade,
The river that is wont to wet your foot
And gives me my new name, who now rejoice
And bask within the shining of your presence.
And were this not the nest where you were born,   10
I would pray heaven to destroy that hill,
To make all desolate, to dry the forest,
Muddy the stream. But I remain and pray,
Dear mirror of my heart, where I am cleansed,
Soon to return and keep your faith to me.   15

136 ❦

Chi mi dará di lagrime un gran fonte,
ch'io sfoghi a pieno il mio dolor immenso,
che m'assale e trafige, quando io penso
al poco amor del mio spietato conte?
  Tosto che 'l sol degli occhi suoi tramonte
agli occhi miei, a' quali è raro accenso,
tanto ha di me non piú memoria o senso,
quanto una tigre del piú aspro monte.
  Ben è 'l mio stato e 'l destín crudo e fero,
ché tosto che da me vi dipartite,
voi cangiate, signor, luogo e pensiero.
  — Io ti scriverò subito — mi dite —
ch'io sarò giunto al loco ove andar chero; —
e poi la vostra fede a me tradite.

136 &

Who will provide me with a copious fountain
Of tears, enough to vent the boundless grief
Which pierces and assails me when I think
How little love my heartless lord bestows?
And when the sunlight of his eyes goes down,   5
From my sad eyes, so seldom lit by his,
He has no more remembrance for my pain
Than would a tiger on the wildest mountain.
My state, my course of life, are harsh and wild,
Because whenever you depart from me,   10
You change your thoughts, my lord, as well as place:
"I will soon write to you," you say to me,
"As soon as I have reached my destination."
But you are never faithful to your promise.

139 ❦

Fiume, che dal mio nome nome prendi,
e bagni i piedi a l'alto colle e vago,
ove nacque il famoso ed alto fago,
de le cui fronde alto disio m'accendi,
    tu vedi spesso lui, spesso l'intendi,
e talor rendi la sua bella imago;
ed a me che d'altr'ombra non m'appago,
cosí sovente, lassa, lo contendi.
    Pur, non ostante che la nobil fronde,
ond'io piansi e cantai con piú d'un verso,
la tua mercé, sí spesso lo nasconde,
    prego 'l ciel ch'altra pioggia o nembo avverso
non turbi, Anasso, mai le tue chiar'onde,
se non quel sol che da quest'occhi verso.

139 ❧

Dear river, who from my name take your own
Who bathe the foothills of that dear high hill
Where that tall, famous beech began to grow,
Tree from whose branch my burning love was born;
You often see him, often hear him speak,   5
And sometimes mirror back his lovely image,
And with me, never pleased by any other,
Too often you contend for his sweet shade.
But notwithstanding that the noble tree,
For which I wept and sang my many verses,   10
Because of you, hides my love from me,
I pray, may never rain nor cloud disturb you,
Anaxus, and may your transparent waves
Never be darkened, save by tears of mine.

142 ❧

Rimandatemi il cor, empio tiranno,
ch'a sí gran torto avete ed istraziate,
e di lui e di me quel proprio fate,
che le tigri e i leon di cerva fanno.
    Son passati otto giorni, a me un anno,
ch'io non ho vostre lettere od imbasciate,
contra le fé che voi m'avete date,
o fonte di valor, conte, e d'inganno.
    Credete ch'io sia Ercol o Sansone
a poter sostener tanto dolore,
giovane e donna e fuor d'ogni ragione,
    massime essendo qui senza 'l mio core
e senza voi a mia difensione,
onde mi suol venir forza e vigore?

142 ❧

O cruel tyrant, give me back my heart
Which you so wrongfully are torturing
And tearing all to pieces, like a lion
Or tiger, preying on an antelope.
Eight days have passed – a year it seems to me –   5
And I have had no word from you, no letter –
Contrary to that oath you swore to me,
O Count, fountain of valor – and deception.
Or do you think I am a Hercules
Or Samson, able to endure such grief –   10
I, a young woman, with small strength of mind,
Now left without my heart, which dwells with you,
Without you to defend me from myself –
You who were wont to be my strength and vigor?

145

Liete campagne, dolci colli ameni,
verdi prati, alte selve, erbose rive,
serrata valle, ov'or soggiorna e vive
chi può far i miei dí foschi e sereni,
    antri d'ombre amorose e fresche pieni,
ove raggio di sol non è ch'arrive,
vaghi augei, chiari fiumi ed aure estive,
vezzose ninfe, Pan, fauni e sileni,
    o rendetemi tosto il mio signore,
voi che l'avete, o fategli almen cónta
la mia pena e l'acerbo aspro dolore:
    ditegli che la vita mia tramonta,
s'omai fra pochi giorni, anzi poch'ore
il sùo raggio a quest'occhi non sormonta.

145 &

O happy country, sweet and smiling hills,
Green meadows, lofty woods and grassy banks,
Valley enclosed, where now he lives and lingers,
Whose power makes my days serene or dark
Caverns of cool and pleasant amorous shades   5
Where ray of daylight never can intrude,
Beautiful birds, clear rivers, summer breezes,
Seductive nymphs, Sileni, Pan and fauns
Restore my lord to me in briefest time,
You who now hold him bound; or at the least   10
Apprise him of my bitter pain, sharp sorrow.
Tell him my life is drawing near its sunset,
Unless in a few days – or, better, hours –
His rays appear to light my weary eyes.

146 ❦

Come posso far pace col desio,
o farvi tregua, poi ch'egli pur vuole,
non essendo qui nosco il suo bel sole,
tranquillo porto e sole al viver mio?
  Egli fa giorno al suo colle natio,
come a chi nulla o poco incresce e duole
o 'l morir nostro o 'l pianto o le parole:
lassa, ch' io nacqui sotto destín rio !
  Lá dove converrá che tosto ceda
a morte l'alma, o tosto a noi ritorni
la beltá ch'al mio mal non par che creda.
  Tal qui, fra questi d'Adria almi soggiorni,
io misera Anassilla, d'Amor preda,
notte e dí chiamo i miei due lumi adorni.

146 ❧

How can I make a truce with my desires,
Or even peace, because he wants me to,
While he is far away from me, my sun,
The tranquil port and sunshine of my life?
He brings the daylight to his native hill   5
Like one who has no sorrows or regrets,
Unmindful of my death, or tears, or words.
Why was I born under so dire a star?
Soon I must give my grieving soul to death,
Unless that beauty soon returns to me –   10
Not seeming to believe in my distress.
Here on these pleasant Adriatic shores
I, wretched Anaxilla, prey of Love,
Call night and day for my two lovely lights.

147 ❧

– Or sopra il forte e veloce destriero –
io dico meco – segue lepre o cerva
il mio bel sole, or rapida caterva
d'uccelli con falconi o con sparviero.

Or assal con lo spiedo il cignal fiero,
quando animoso il suo venir osserva;
or a l'opre di Marte, or di Minerva
rivolge l'alto e saggio suo pensiero.

Or mangia, or dorme, or leva ed or ragiona,
or vagheggia il suo colle, or con l'umana
sua maniera trattiene ogni persona. –

Cosí, signor, bench'io vi sia lontana,
sí fattamente Amor mi punge e sprona,
ch'ogni vostr'opra m'è presente e piana.

147 ﷼

I tell myself I see my lovely sun
Mounted upon his powerful, swift steed,
Chasing the hare or hart, or rapid flock
Of birds, with falcon or with sparrowhawk;
Now with his spear he fights the savage boar,   5
Awaiting its attack with fierce disdain;
Again, he bends his wise and lofty thoughts
To the pursuits of Mars and of Minerva.
He eats now, now he sleeps, he rises, speaks,
Now gazes on his hill, now with humane   10
Welcoming manner he receives all guests.
And so, my lord, though I am far away,
Love so inspires me and spurs me on
That I can plainly see your every act.

150 🪶

Larghe vene d'umor, vive scintille,
che m'ardete e bagnate in acqua e 'n fiamma,
sí che di me omai non resta dramma,
che non sia tutta pelaghi e faville,
    fate che senta almeno una di mille
aspre mie pene chi mi lava e 'nfiamma,
né di foco che m'arda sente squamma,
né d'umor goccia che dagli occhi stille.
    – Non son – mi dice Amor – le ragion pari;
egli è nobile e bel, tu brutta e vile;
egli larghi, tu hai li cieli avari.
    Gioia e tormento al merto tuo simile
convien ch'io doni. – In questi stati vari
io peno, ei gode; Amor segue suo stile.

150 🦎

Large streams of liquid, scintillating sparks
Burning and drowning me in fire and water,
Till not one tiny grain of me is left
That is not turned to oceans and to flames –
Make him at least feel one among the thousand   5
Of these sharp pains that drown me and inflame me,
At least one flake of all the fire that burns me,
Or one small drop of water from his eyes.
Love says: "The scales between you are not even.
He's handsome, noble; you, ugly, low-born.   10
And Fate was kind to him, stingy to you.
Torment and joy I give as each deserves it
In your opposing states." So I must suffer,
He must rejoice. Love follows his own ways.

151 🦂

Piangete, donne, e con voi pianga Amore,
poi che non piange lui, che m'ha ferita
sí, che l'alma fará tosto partita
da questo corpo tormentato fuore.
  E, se mai da pietoso e gentil core
l'estrema voce altrui fu essaudita,
dapoi ch'io sarò morta e sepelita,
scrivete la cagion del mio dolore:
  "Per amar molto ed esser poco amata
visse e morí infelice, ed or qui giace
la piú fidel amante che sia stata.
  Pregale, viator, riposo e pace,
ed impara da lei, sí mal trattata,
a non seguir un cor crudo e fugace."

151 ᚕ

Weep, Ladies, and let Love join in your grief.
He does not weep, who wounded me so sore
That soon my soul will take its final leave
From this tormented and afflicted body.
If ever a compassionate, gentle heart   5
Should grant a loving woman's dying wish,
When, dead and cold, I in my grave shall lie,
Write down the reasons for my early death:
"Loving too much, loved little in return,
She lived and died unhappy, who now lies   10
Here, the most loyal lover of all times.
Pray for her soul's repose, good passer-by,
And learn from her, who was so badly used,
Never to love one cruel and untrue."

152 🙞

Io vorrei pur ch'Amor dicesse come
debbo seguirlo, e con qual arte e stile
possa sperar di far chi m'arde umíle,
o diporr'io queste amorose some.
    Io ho le forze omai sí fiacche e dome,
sí paventosa son tornata e vile,
che, quasi ad Eco imagine simile,
di donna serbo sol la voce e 'l nome;
    né, perché le vestigia del mio sole
io segua sempre, come fece anch'ella,
e risponda a l'estreme sue parole,
    posso indur la mia fiera e dura stella
ad oprar sí ch'ei, crudo come suole,
s'arresti al suon di mia stanca favella.

152 ❧

I wish that Love could only tell me how
I best could follow him, what art or style,
Could make him humble, who so makes me burn,
Or how to rid me of the weight of love.
My forces are so weakened, so brought low,   5
So fearful I've become, and such a coward,
That I've become an image of fair Echo,
Keeping the voice and name alone of woman.
Not even if I follow in the footsteps
Of my belovèd sun, as Echo did,   10
And always answer him with his last words,
Can I persuade my proud and stubborn fate
To move him – cruel as he's wont to be –
To pause upon the sound of my weak voice.

155 🐝

Due anni e piú ha giá voltato il cielo,
ch'io restai presa a l'amoroso visco
per una beltá tal, che, dirlo ardisco,
simil mai non si vide in mortal velo:
    per questo io la divolgo, e non la celo,
e non mi pento, anzi glorio e gioisco;
e, se donna giamai gradí, gradisco
questa fiamma amorosa e questo gelo;
    e duolmi sol, se sará mai quell'ora,
che da me si disciolga e leghi altronde
la beltá ch'ogni cosa arde e inamora.
    E, se Morte a chi prega unqua risponde,
la prego che permetta, anzi ch'io mora,
che non vegga d'altrui l'amata fronde.

155 ❧

Two years and more the heavens have revolved
Since I was captured in the snare of love
By such great beauty that – I dare to say –
The like was never seen in mortal veil.
This I can plainly say and not conceal   5
And not repent; I glory and rejoice –
As much as any woman ever did –
In both the vivid flame and ice of love.
I'd only grieve if there should be a time
When my lord's beauty, which enamors all,   10
Detached from me, should bind him to another.
And if Death ever answers any prayers,
I beg Her not to let me, during life,
See my lord tied in bondage to another.

159 ❧

Quella febre amorosa, che m'atterra
due anni e piú, e quel gravoso incarco
ch'io sento, poi ch'Amor mi prese al varco
di duo begli occhi, onde l'uscir mi serra,
    potea bastare a farmi andar sotterra,
lasciar lo spirto del suo corpo scarco,
senza voler ch'oltra i suoi strali e l'arco,
altra febre, altro mal mi fesse guerra.
    Padre del ciel, tu vedi in quante pene
questo misero spirto e questa scorza
a tormentare Amor e febre viene.
    Di queste febri o l'una o l'altra smorza,
ché due tanti nemici non sostiene
donna sí frale e di sí poca forza.

159 ❧

Fever of love, which for two years and over
Has pinned me to the earth, and the great burden
I feel, since Love has caught me in his ambush
By two fine eyes, which I cannot escape,
Would be enough to drive me to the grave,   5
Leaving my soul disburdened of its body,
Without the need of any other arrows,
Of fever, or disease to war upon me.
Father of heaven, You see with what pains
Love comes, along with fever, both tormenting   10
This miserable frame and its weak spirit.
Destroy one of the fevers, or the other!
For I, frail woman, with so little force,
Cannot fight off two such strong enemies.

161 ❧

Verso il bel nido, ove restai partendo,
ove vive di me la miglior parte,
quando il sol faticoso torna e parte,
mai sempre l'ale del disir io stendo.
    E me ad or ad or biasmo e riprendo,
ch'a star con voi non usai forza ed arte,
sapendo che, da voi stando in disparte,
ben mille volte al dì moro vivendo.
    La speme mosse il mio dubbioso piede,
che deveste venir tosto a vedermi,
per arrestar questa fugace vita.
    Osservate, signor, la data fede:
fate, venendo, questi lidi, or ermi,
cari e gioiosi, e me lieta e gradita.

161 ❧

Toward that sweet nest where I remained though
   parting,
And where the better part of me still lingers,
Whether the weary sun returns or leaves,
I always spread the wings of my desire.
And still from time to time I blame myself   5
For never having used device or force
To stay with you, knowing, away from you,
A thousand times a day I die while living.
My doubtful feet were moved by constant hope
That you would follow soon to visit me,   10
Extend my fleeting life a little longer.
Observe, my lord, the promise you have given:
To come and make these dreary shores alive,
Joyous and loved, and me grateful and happy.

164 ❧

Occhi miei lassi, non lasciate il pianto,
come non lascian me téma e spavento
di veder tosto a noi rubato e spento
il lume ch'amo e riverisco tanto.
  Pregate morte, se si può, fra tanto
che mi venga essa a cavar fuor di stento;
perché morir a un tratto è men tormento,
che viver sempre a mille morti a canto.
  Io direi che pregaste prima Amore
che facesse cangiar voglia e pensiero
al nostro crudo e disleal signore;
  ma so che saria invan, perché sí fiero,
cosí indurato ed ostinato core
non ebbe mai illustre cavaliero.

164 🙋

My weary eyes, don't ever cease to weep,
Since I am never free from trembling fear,
Fear I shall see the light I love and cherish
Stolen from me and quenched, and that too soon.
Sad eyes of mine, pray Death, if it may be,   5
To come to me and save me from this state,
Because to die at once is lesser torment
Than to live on among a thousand deaths.
First I desire you to pray to Love
To make my cruel and unfaithful lord   10
Change his desires and his ways of thought.
I know this would be vain; he has so proud,
Hardened and obstinate a heart within him,
As never high-born knight possessed before.

166 ᷧ

Io accuso talora Amor e lui
ch'io amo: Amor, che mi legò sí forte;
lui, che mi può dar vita e dammi morte,
cercando tôrsi a me per darsi altrui;
    ma, meglio avista, poi scuso ambedui,
ed accuso me sol de la mia sorte,
e le mie voglie al voler poco accorte,
ch' io de le pene mie ministra fui.
    Perché, vedendo la mia indegnitade,
devea mirar in men gradito loco,
per poteme sperar maggior pietade.
    Fetonte, Icaro ed io, per poter poco
ed osar molto, in questa e quella etade
restiamo estinti da troppo alto foco.

166 &

I accuse Love, and equally accuse
Him whom I love: Love who bound me so fast,
And him who can give life to me, or death,
Who steals from me to win another's love.
But now, wiser at last, both I excuse,   5
Accuse myself alone for my hard fate,
And since my wishes were too ill-advised,
I see I was the minister of my grief.
Because, when I regard my low estate,
I know I should have sought a humbler place   10
Where I might hope to have received more pity.
Phaethon, Icarus, and I dared much,
But little did we do: we – in that age
And this – have been destroyed by that high fire.

167 ❧

Poi che disia cangiar pensiero e voglia
l'empio signor, ch'onoro ed amo tanto,
senza curar de' fiumi del mio pianto,
e del mancar de la mia frale spoglia,

io prego morte, che di qua mi toglia,
perché non abbia questo crudo il vanto;
o prego Amor, che mi rallenti alquanto,
poi che de' doni suoi tutta mi spoglia;

sí che o morta non vegga tanto danno,
o viva e sciolta non lo stimi molto,
allor che gli occhi altro mirar sapranno.

Dunque o sia falso il mio temere e stolto,
o resti sciolta al rinovar de l'anno,
o queti il corpo in bel marmo sepolto.

167

Since my unfaithful lord will change his mind
And pay no heed to all my floods of tears
Nor to the failing of my fragile body,
I plead with Death to carry me away
So that this evil one may not take pleasure   5
In seeing my decline. I pray to Love
To cool my passion, for he takes again
All of the gifts that he once gave to me –
So that, in death, I may not feel my harm,
Or if alive I may not care so much,   10
Or I may find another one to love.
Then, may my fears be foolish and unfounded,
Or may my heart be free beyond this year,
Or may my body rest in marble tomb.

171 ❦

Voi potete, signor, ben tôrmi voi
con quel cor d'indurato diamante,
e farvi d'altra donna novo amante:
di che cosa non è, che piú m'annoi;
    ma non potete giá ritôrmi poi
l'imagin vostra, il vostro almo sembiante,
che giorno e notte mi sta sempre innante,
poi che mi fece Amor de' servi suoi;
    non potete ritôrmi quei desiri,
che m'acceser di voi sí caldamente,
il foco, il pianto, che per gli occhi verso.
    Questi mi fien ne' miei gravi martíri
dolce sostegno, e la memoria ardente
del diletto provato, c'han disperso.

171 ❧

You can, my lord, steal yourself from my side
With your unyielding heart of adamant,
And make yourself another lady's lover –
No other thing would torture me so much.
But one thing you can never steal from me,   5
The image of your glorious countenance
Which day and night appears before my eyes
Since Love has counted me among his servants.
You cannot steal from me those strong desires
That you so blazingly kindled in me.   10
The fire, the tears that pour out of my eyes,
May these be always sweet supports for me
Among my pains: the ardent memory
Of joy once felt, that cannot be dissolved.

172 ❧

S'una candida fede, un cor sincero,
una gran riverenza, una infinita
voglia a servir altrui pronta ed ardita,
un servo grato al suo signor mai fèro,

devrebbe pur, signor, l'affetto vero
e la mia fede esser da voi gradita,
se i vostri onor piú cari che la vita
mi fûr mai sempre, e piú ch'oro ed impero.

Ma poi che mia fortuna mi contende
mercé sí giusta, poi che a sí gran torto
a schivo il servir mio da voi si prende,

ciò ch'a voi piace paziente porto,
sperando pur che Dio, che tutto intende,
vi faccia un dí de la mia fede accorto.

172 ❧

If candid faith and a devoted heart,
Great reverence, an infinite desire
To serve another promptly and with zeal
Has ever made a servant please his master,
My true affection ought to do, my lord,   5
And my fidelity should also please you,
Because your honor is more dear to me
Than life itself, far more than gold and power.
But since my fortune steals away from me
So just a recompense, and you, so wrongly   10
And grudgingly accept my loving service,
I patiently will bear what you desire,
Hoping that God, Who understands all things,
One day will make you mindful of my faith.

174 ❧

Una inaudita e nova crudeltate,
un esser al fuggir pronto e leggiero,
un andar troppo di sue lodi altero,
un tôrre ad altri la sua libertate,
  un vedermi penar senza pietate,
un aver sempre a' miei danni il pensiero,
un rider di mia morte quando pèro,
un aver voglie ognor fredde e gelate,
  un eterno timor di lontananza,
un verno eterno senza primavera,
un non dar giamai cibo a la speranza
  m'han fatto divenir una Chimera,
uno abisso confuso, un mar, ch'avanza
d'onde e tempeste una marina vera.

174 ❧

A new unheard-of cruelty! So quick
And light of foot was he to make escape,
Walking too proudly in his noble gifts,
Stealing her freedom from another one…
Seeing me suffer without any pity,   5
And thinking always how to give me pain,
Laughing about my death – while I am dying –
His wishes ever cold as solid ice.
Eternal fear of distances between us,
An everlasting winter with no spring,   10
Not ever giving any food for hope…
All this has made me turn to a Chimera,
Confused abyss, a sea forever raging
With waves and tempests on a lonely beach.

175 ❧

Quasi uom che rimaner de' tosto senza
il cibo, oncle nudrir suol la sua vita,
piú dell'usato a prenderne s'aita,
fin che gli è presso posto in sua presenza;
   convien ch' innanzi a l'aspra dipartenza
ch'a sí crudi digiuni l'alma invita,
ella piú de l'usato sia nodrita,
per poter poi soffrir sí dura assenza.
   Però, vaghi occhi miei, mirate fiso
piú de l'usato, anzi bevete il bene
e 'l bel del vostro amato e caro viso.
   E voi, orecchie, oltra l'usato piene
restate del parlar, ché 'l paradiso
certo armonia piú dolce non contiene.

175

As one who soon must lose the precious food
Which used to be the sole stay of her life,
Will help herself to more than was her custom
Whenever it is placed before her eye,
Just so my soul, before this bitter parting   5
Foretelling so prolonged and harsh a fast,
Takes to herself more nourishment than ever
Hoping to bear the absence soon to come.
Therefore, my eager eyes, gaze without moving,
More than you used, to drink in your reward,   10
The dear and lovely face of your belovèd;
And ears, more than you ever used to do,
Wait on his words, for even paradise
Cannot produce a lovelier harmony.

179 ❧

Meraviglia non è, se 'n uno istante
ritraeste da me pensieri e voglie,
ché vi venne cagion di prender moglie,
e divenir marito, ov'eri amante.
    Nodo e fé, che non è stretto e costante,
per picciola cagion si rompe e scioglie:
la mia fede e 'l mio nodo il vanto toglie
al nodo gordiano ed al diamante.
    Però non fia giamai che scioglia guesto
e rompa quella, se non cruda morte,
la qual prego, signor, che venga presto;
    sí ch'io non vegga con le luci scorte
quello ch'or col pensier atro e funesto
mi fa veder la mia spietata sorte.

179 ❧

It is no wonder if in one brief moment
You have withdrawn from me thought and desire,
For you've decided now to take a wife
And be a husband, as you were a lover.
A knot, a faith, which are not fixed and constant,   5
Will break, or be dissolved, for little cause;
But my own faith, my knot, will steal the honors
Both from the Gordian knot, and adamant.
And so it will not happen that one loosens,
The other shatters, unless cruel Death   10
– Whom now I pray, my lord, quickly to come –
Keeps me from seeing with my outward eye
Whatever adverse Fortune now compels me
To gaze on with my ruinous, dark mind.

187 ❧

Se gran temenza non tenesse a freno
la mia lingua bramosa e 'l mio disio,
sí ch'io potessi dire al signor mio
come amando e temendo io vengo meno,

io spererei che quel di grazie pieno
viso leggiadro, onde tutt'altro oblio,
quant'è 'l mio stato travagliato e rio,
tanto lo fesse un dí chiaro e sereno;

e quello, onde m'avinse e strinse, nodo
non cercherebbe, lassa, di slegarlo,
allor che piú credea che fosse sodo.

Ma per troppo timor non oso farlo:
cosí dentro al mio cor mi struggo e rodo,
e sol con meco e con Amor ne parlo.

187 ❧

If my great fear did not impose restraint
Upon my eager tongue and my desire,
I could with frankness say to my dear lord
How weak I have become from love and dread –
Then I might hope that his enchanting face,   5
– Whose charm makes me forget all other men –
Would come to make me happy and serene,
As much as now my state is sad and weary.
And that the knot with which he holds me bound
He would not try to loosen or untie   10
Just when I thought that it was firmly fastened.
But since from too much fear I don't dare speak,
Within me I consume and gnaw my heart,
And only speak to Love and to myself.

192 &

Amor, lo stato tuo è proprio quale
è una ruota, che mai sempre gira,
e chi v'è suso or canta ed or sospira,
e senza mai fermarsi or scende or sale.
   Or ti chiama fedele, or disleale;
or fa pace con teco, ed or s'adira;
ora ti si dá in preda, or si ritira;
or nel ben teme, ed or spera nel male;
      or s'alza al cielo, or cade ne l'inferno;
or è lunge dal lido, or giunge in porto;
or trema a mezza state, or suda il verno.
   Io, lassa me, nel mio maggior conforto
sono assalita d'un sospetto interno,
che mi tien sempre il cor fra vivo e morto.

192 &

Love, I imagine you as like a wheel
Forever turning, as it never stops.
Those on the top now sing and later sigh,
As, without pause, they're carried up and down.
Now they will call you faithful and then false,   5
Now they're at peace with you, and now they're
    angry,
And sometimes they surrender, sometimes flee.
When things go well, they fear; when badly, hope.
Now they are raised to heaven, fall to hell.
Now far from shore, now coming into port;   10
They shiver in the summer, sweat in winter.
And I, uneasy in my greatest joy,
Am overcome by a deep inward fear
That holds me ever between life and death.

197 ❧

Chi 'l crederia? Felice era il mio stato,
quando a vicenda or doglia ed or diletto,
or téma, or speme m'ingombrava il petto,
e m'era il cielo or chiaro ed or turbato;
    perché questo d'Amor fiorito prato
non è a mio giudicio a pien perfetto,
se non è misto di contrario effetto,
quando la noia fa il piacer piú grato.
    Ma or l'ha pieno sí di spine e sterpi
chi lo può fare, e svelti i fiori e l'erba,
che sol v'albergan venenosi serpi.
    O fé cangiata, o mia fortuna acerba!
Tu le speranze mie recidi e sterpi:
la cagion dentro al petto mio si serba.

197 ♈

Who could believe it? Happy was my state
When turn by turn, now pain, and now delight,
Now fear, now hope, possessed my loving heart.
The sky was clear one moment, dark the next,
Because the flowery meadow filled with Love   5
Is, in my judgment, never fully ripe
Unless composed of contrary effects:
Then pain, by contrast, will enhance delight.
But now the one who has the vital power
Has filled that meadow with harsh weeds
     and thorns,   10
Making it only fit for poisonous snakes.
Oh, faith transformed, and oh, my bitter fortune!
You have cut down and rooted out my hopes.
The cause, this love, still lives within my heart.

199 ❧

Signor, ite felice ove 'l disio
ad or ad or piú chiaro vi richiama
a far volar al ciel la vostra fama,
secura da la morte e da l'oblio;
    ricordatevi sol come rest'io,
solinga tortorella in secca rama,
che senza lui, che sol sospira e brama,
fugge ogni verde pianta e chiaro rio.
    Al mio cor fate cara compagnia,
il vostro ad altra donna non donate,
poi che a me sí fedel nol deste pria.
    Sopra tutto tornar vi ricordate,
e, s'avien che fia quando estinta io sia,
de la mia rara fé non vi scordate.

199 ❧

My lord, go happily where your desire
Appeals to you more clearly day by day,
To make your fame fly upward to the sky,
Securely past oblivion and death.
Remember only how I stay behind,   5
A lonely little dove on a dry branch,
Avoiding all green plants and limpid streams,
Bereft of him she sighs for and desires.
Be still a dear companion to my heart
And do not give your heart to any other –   10
You never gave it faithfully to me.
Above all else, remember to return.
And if you find I am already dead,
Do not forget my rare fidelity.

202 ?⅘

Poi che per mio destín volgeste in parte
piedi e voler, onde perdei la spene
di riveder piú mai quelle serene
luci, ch'o giá lodate in tante carte,
    io mi volsi al gran Sole, e con quell'arte
e quella luce, che da lui sol viene,
trassi fuor da le sirti e da l'arene
il legno mio per via di remi e sarte.
    La ragion fu le sarte, e i remi fûro
la volontá, che a l' ira ed a l'orgoglio
d'Amor si fece poi argine e muro.
    Cosí, senza temer di dar in scoglio,
mi vivo in porto omai queto e sicuro;
d'un sol mi lodo, e di nessun mi doglio.

202 ❧

Since, owing to ill fate, you've turned from me
Your feet and your desire I've lost all hope
Ever to see again your serene eyes,
Which I have praised in many a loving poem.
I have turned back to the great Sun above,   5
And with that light that comes from Him alone
I have brought out through treacherous reefs and
    sands
My little ship, by means of oars and sails.
Reason became my sails, my will the oars,
Forming for me a solid dike and wall   10
Against the fatal wrath and pride of Love.
Thus without any fear of shoals or rocks,
I live in this serene and blessed harbor.
I praise One only, and I grieve for none.

207 ❧

Poi che m'hai resa, Amor, la libertade,
mantiemmi in questo dolce e lieto stato,
sí che 'l mio cor sia mio, sí come è stato
ne la mia prima giovenil etade;
    o, se pur vuoi che dietro a le tue strade,
amando, segua il mio costume usato,
fa' ch'io arda di foco piú temprato,
e che, s'io ardo, altrui n'abbia pietade;
    perché mi par veder, a certi segni,
che ordisci novi lacci e nove faci,
e di ritrarmi al giogo tuo t'ingegni.
    Serbami, Amor, in queste brevi paci,
Amor, che contra me superbo regni,
Amor, che nel mio mal sol ti compiaci.

207 ❧

Since you, O Love, have given back my freedom,
Keep me forever in this happy state,
So that my heart's my own, as once it was
In my first youthful years of carefree joy.
Or if you wish me still to tread your ways   5
In loving, following you, as I once did,
Then let me burn with a less ardent flame,
Or, burning, let it be for one who loves me.
For now I seem to see by certain signs
That you are laying down new traps for me,   10
New flames, new ropes to bind me to your yoke.
Save for me, Love, this present short-lived peace,
Love, who so haughtily rules over me,
Love, who takes pleasure only in my pain.

208 ⁊

Amor m'ha fatto tal ch'io vivo in foco,
qual nova salamandra al mondo, e quale
l'altro di lei non men stranio animale,
che vive e spira nel medesmo loco.
    Le mie delizie son tutte e 'l mio gioco
viver ardendo e non sentire il male,
e non curar ch'ei che m'induce a tale
abbia di me pietá molto né poco.
    A pena era anche estinto il primo ardore,
che accese l'altro Amore, a quel ch'io sento
fin qui per prova, piú vivo e maggiore.
    Ed io d'arder amando non mi pento,
pur che chi m'ha di novo tolto il core
resti de l'arder mio pago e contento.

208 ❧

Love has made me live in ceaseless fire
Like a strange salamander come to earth
Or like that bird of fable, no less strange,
That lives and breathes in this same element.
All my delight it is, and all my joy,   5
To live, endlessly burning, with no pain,
Not caring whether he who caused my grief
Takes pity on me, either great or small.
Barely had I put out my heart's first flame
Than Love kindled a second, which I feel   10
As sharper, livelier than the first had been.
This ardency of love I don't repent,
So long as he who lit my heart anew
Remains at peace, contented in my love.

209 🦋

Io non veggio giamai giunger quel giorno,
ove nacque Colui che carne prese,
essendo Dio, per scancellar l'offese
del nostro padre al suo Fattor ritorno,
    che non mi risovenga il modo adorno,
col quale, avendo Amor le reti tese
fra due begli occhi ed un riso, mi prese:
occhi, ch'or fan da me lunge soggiorno:
    e de l'antico amor qualche puntura
io non senta al desire ed al cor darmi,
sí fu la piaga mia profonda e dura.
    E, se non che ragion pur prende l'armi
e vince il senso, questa acerba cura
sarebbe or tal che non potrebbe aitarmi.

209 ?❧

I never see that day when He was born
Who took upon Himself our human flesh,
Though being God, to cancel the offenses
Of the first man, who sinned against his Maker,
But I remember the delightful way   5
In which Love spread his nets to capture me
With two fine eyes and one appealing smile,
Eyes, which now stay away from me too long;
And feel besides the sting of former love
Stabbing my heart again with sharp desire,   10
Because the wound it made had been so deep.
And, were it not that Reason takes up arms
To conquer Sense, this bitter care of mine
Would be such that I could not help myself.

210 ❧

Veggio Amor tender l'arco, e novo strale
por ne la corda e saettarmi il core,
e, non ben saldo ancor l'altro dolore,
nova piaga rifarmi e novo male;
   e sí il suo foco m'è proprio e fatale,
sí son preda e mancipio ognor d'Amore,
che, perché l'alma vegga il suo migliore,
ripararsi da lui né vuol né vale.
   Ben è ver che la tela, che m'ordisce,
sempre è di ricco stame; e quindi aviene
che ne' suoi danni il cor père e gioisce;
   e 'l ferro è tale, onde a ferirmi or viene,
che si può dir che chi per lui perisce
prova sol una vita e sommo bene.

210 ?

I see Love bend his bow, and on the string
Set a new arrow aimed to pierce my heart,
Wanting, while my first wound is not yet healed,
To give me a new wound, a second evil;
And since his fire is so inborn in me,   5
I am the prey and slave of Love forever;
And though my soul knows what is best for her,
She neither can nor will escape from him.
In spite of all, the rare web that he weaves
Is of so rich a texture that my heart,   10
When caught in it, rejoices while it dies.
Likewise the arrow on its way to wound me
Is such that any one who's struck by it,
Can only feel life and the highest good.

211 ❦

Qual sagittario, che sia sempre avezzo
trarre ad un segno, e mai colpo non falla,
o da propria vaghezza tratto o dalla
spene c'ha da ritrarne onore e prezzo,
    Amor, che nel mio mal mai non è sezzo,
torna a ferirmi il cor, né mai si stalla,
e la piaga or risalda apre e rifalla;
né mi val s'io 'l temo o s'io lo sprezzo.
    Tanto di me ferir diletto prende,
e tal n'attende e merca onor, ch'omai,
per quel ch'io provo, ad altro non intende.
    Il vivo foco, ond'io arsi e cantai
molti anni, a pena è spento, che raccende
d'un altro il cor, che tregua non ha mai.

211 ⊰

Like a skilled archer, one who is accustomed
To aiming at his target, never missing,
Drawn by his eagerness and constant hope
Of winning honor or a worthy prize,
Love, who is never last to do me harm,   5
Returns to strike my heart, then strikes again,
The wound once healed he opens up afresh.
Nor does it help to fear or to defy him.
He takes such pleasure every time he wounds me,
Expecting to obtain a rich reward   10
In what I feel – he cares for nothing else.
The lively fire for which I burned and sang
Those many years is so near-spent, that Love
Now lights a new one, giving me no truce.

213 ❧

Un veder tôrsi a poco a poco il core,
misera, e non dolersi de l'offesa;
un veder chiaro la sua fiamma accesa
negli altrui lumi e non fuggir l'ardore;
  un cercar volontario d'uscir fore
de la sua libertá poco anzi resa;
un aver sempre a l'altrui voglia intesa
l'alma vaga e ministra al suo dolore;
  un parer tutto grazia e leggiadria
ciò che si vede in un aspetto umano,
se parli o taccia, o se si mova o stia,
  son le cagion ch'io temo non pian piano
cada nel mar del pianto, ov'era pria,
la vita mia; e prego Dio che 'nvano.

213 ❧

To see, little by little, how your heart
Is stolen, and to utter no complaint,
Clearly to see his flame burning anew
In other's eyes, and not desert one's love,
To seek by one's own will to walk away   5
From liberty possessed a while before,
And always to surrender to his will –
A soul forever minister to grief –
Always to seem pure grace and elegance
As much as can be seen in human face,   10
In speaking or in silence, still or moving –
These are the causes why I fear – not slowly –
To fall into a sea of tears, as once
My life was; and I pray to God in vain.

214 ❧

La piaga, ch'io credea che fosse salda
per la omai molta assenzia e poco amore
di quell'alpestro ed indurato core,
freddo piú che di neve fredda falda,
    si desta ad or ad ora e si riscalda,
e gitta ad or ad or sangue ed umore;
sí che l'alma si vive anco in timore,
ch'esser devrebbe omai sicura e balda.
    Né, perché cerchi agiunger novi lacci
al collo mio, so far che molto o poco
quell'antico mio nodo non m'impacci.
    Si suol pur dir che foco scaccia foco;
ma tu, Amor, che 'l mio martír procacci,
fai che questo in me, lassa, or non ha loco.

214 ﷼

The wound which I believed to have been healed
By the long absence and the little love
Shown by that alpine and indurate heart,
Colder than any drift of snow is cold,
Has wakened once again and now grows hot   5
And casts forth once again both blood and water,
So that my spirit lives again in fear,
Although by now it should be brave and bold.
Nor, though I seek to add to my old yoke
New bonds, can I do very much or little   10
To keep that old knot from impeding me.
It's often said that "fire casts out fire,"
But you, O Love, you who have caused my torment
Keep the new love from taking root in me.

216 ❧

D'esser sempre ésca al tuo cocente foco
e sempre segno a' tuoi pungenti strali,
d'esser sempre ministra de' miei mali
ed aver sempre i miei tormenti a gioco,

io non mi doglio, Amor, molto né poco,
poi che dal dí, che 'l desir prese l'ali,
mi son fatti i martír propri e fatali,
e libertade in me non ha piú loco.

Pur che tu mi conservi in questo stato,
dov'or m'hai posta, e sotto quel signore,
onde il cor novamente m'hai legato,

o mi fia dolce, o tornerá minore
quanto son per provar, quanto ho provato
la sua rara bellezza e 'l suo valore.

216 ❧

Always to be the flint of your hot fire,
Always the target of your stinging arrows,
Always to be my minister of sorrow,
Always to have my torment made a game,
Of this I don't complain, Love, much or little,   5
Since from that day when my desire took wing,
I made these fateful tortures for myself
And freedom can no longer dwell in me.
If you, O Love, keep me where you have placed me
Subjected to that lord, to whom you've bound me   10
Tying my heart with knots in the same way,
Either his valor or his wondrous beauty
Will turn to sweetness, or become less grave
Because of all the pain I have endured.

221 ❧

A mezzo il mare, ch'io varcai tre anni
fra dubbi venti, ed era quasi in porto,
m'ha ricondotta Amor, che a sí gran torto
è ne' travagli miei pronto e ne' danni;
　e per doppiare a' miei disiri i vanni
un sí chiaro oriente agli occhi ha pòrto,
che, rimirando lui, prendo conforto,
e par che manco il travagliar m'affanni.
　Un foco eguale al primo foco io sento,
e, se in sí poco spazio questo è tale,
che de l'altro non sia maggior, pavento.
　Ma che poss'io, se m'è l'arder fatale,
se volontariamente andar consento
d'un foco in altro, e d'un in altro male?

221 ⦓

Far out at sea, where I have sailed three years
Among disastrous winds, now close to port,
Love, to my great distress, has forced me back,
Unjust, swift to inflict distress and grief!
And, to give double wings to my desire,   5
Has held so fair a dawn before my eyes,
That seeing it again, I take new comfort,
Not feeling even weariness or pain.
A fire I feel, equal to my first flame,
And if this has occurred in such short time,   10
I fear it may be stronger than the first.
What can I do, if burning is my fate,
And I consent to go, of my own will,
From one fierce fire, one evil, to the next?

224 ✎

L'empio tuo strale, Amore,
è piú crudo e piú forte
assai che quel di Morte;
ché per Morte una volta sol si more,
e tu col tuo colpire
uccidi mille, e non si può morire.
Dunque, Amore, è men male
la morte che 'l tuo strale.

224 ❧

Your cruel arrow, Love,
Is sharper and more dire
Even than Death's own dart
Because through Death one simply dies one time,
While you, when you attack   5
Can strike a thousand times, yet never slay.
So, Love, your piercing dart,
Is deadlier than Death.

229 🦋

Qual fosse il mio martíre
nel vostro dipartire,
voi 'l potete di qui, signor, stimare,
che mi fu tolto infin il lagrimare.
E l'umor, che, per gli occhi uscendo fore,
suol sfogarmi 'l dolore,
in quell'amara e cruda dipartita
mi negò la sua aita.
O mio misero stato,
d'altra donna non mai visto o provato,
poi che quello, ond'Amor è sí cortese,
nel maggior uopo a me sola contese!

229 ❧

When we were forced to part
The pain that pierced my heart
You can imagine, sir, for you can see
That the relief of tears was barred from me.
The water that once, pouring from my eyes   5
Used to relieve my sighs,
Now, in this cruel, bitter separation
Withheld its consolation
Alas, my grievous woe!
No other lady ever felt it so,   10
Since that release Love granted me before,
In my most need he lets me use no more.

230 ❧

Signor, per cortesia,
non mi dite che, quand'andaste via,
Amor mi negò 'l pianto
perché, vedendo in me giá spento il foco,
l'acqua non v'avea loco
per temperarlo alquanto;
anzi dite piú tosto che fu tanto
in quel punto l'ardore,
che diseccò l'umore;
e non potei mostrare
l'acerba pena mia col lagrimare,
per ciò che 'l corpo mio, d'ogni umor casso,
o restò tutto foco, o tutto sasso.

230 ?&

My lord, in courtesy,
Don't say to me, that when you went away
Love did not let me weep
Because, my fire of love having burnt out,
There was no need for water   5
To cool my passion's heat:
Say rather that my ardor at that moment
Blazed with so fierce a flame
That it dried up all moisture,
And so I could not show you   10
My bitter pain by weeping copious tears,
Because my body, robbed of all its humors,
Must have remained all fire – or all stone.

231 ❧

Le pene de l'inferno insieme insieme,
appresso il mio gran foco,
tutte son nulla o poco;
perch'ove non è speme
l'anima risoluta al patir sempre
s'avezza al duol, che mai non cangia tempre.
La mia è maggior noia,
perché gusto talor ombra di gioia
mercé de la speranza;
e questa varia usanza
di gioir e patire
fa maggior il martire.

231 �

The pains of hell heaped all together
Compared to my great fire
Are little – almost nothing –
For where there is no hope,
The soul, resolved to suffer on forever,   5
Grows used to pain which never can be changed.
Mine is the greater sorrow
Because it tasted once a shade of joy,
Thanks to the gift of hope.
This constant interchange   10
Of suffering and joy
Increases my pain ever.

232 ❧

Se 'l cibo, onde i suoi servi nutre Amore,
è 'l dolore e 'l martíre,
come poss'io morire
nodrita dal dolore?
Il semplicetto pesce,
che solo ne l'umor vive e respira,
in un momento spira
tosto che de l'acqua esce;
e l'animal, che vive in fiamma e 'n foco,
muor, come cangia loco.
Or, se tu voi ch'io moia,
Amor, trammi di guai e pommi in gioia;
perché col pianto, mio cibo vitale,
tu non mi puoi far male.

232 ��

If that with which Love nourishes his servants
Is suffering and pain,
How can I ever die
Nourished so well by pain?
The simple little fish   5
Who only lives and breathes in flowing water
Will die immediately
As soon as he is taken from the water.
And that strange beast who lives and breathes in fire
Dies in another place.   10
So, if you wish me dead,
O Love, take me from pain and give me joy
Because with tears which are my vital food
I never can be harmed.

233 ❧

Beato insogno e caro,
che sotto oscuro velo m'hai mostrato
il mio felice stato,
qual potrá ingegno chiaro,
quant'io debbo e vorrei, giamai lodarte
in vive voci o 'n carte?
Io per me farò fede,
dovunque essser potrá mia voce udita,
che, sol la tua mercede,
io son restata in vita.

233 ≈

Dearest and blessèd dream
You who have shown me under dusky veil
My fortune-favored state,
How could the highest mind
Ever portray you as I ought to do   5
In song or else on paper?
I shall make men believe –
Wherever in the world my voice is heard –
That only by your mercy
Have I remained alive.   10

235 ❧

Conte, dov'è andata
la fé sí tosto, che m'avete data?
Che vuol dir che la mia
è piú costante, che non era pria?
Che vuol dir che, da poi
che voi partiste, io son sempre con voi?
Sapete voi quel che dirá la gente,
dove forza d'Amor punto si sente?
– O che conte crudele!
o che donna fedele!

235 ❧

Count, where has fled so soon
The faithful love that once you swore to me?
What does it mean that mine
Is still more constant than it was before?
What does it mean that since   5
You left me, I am always at your side?
Do you know, sir, what other people say
Who never felt the sharpened stab of love?
Oh, what a cruel lord!
Oh, what a loyal lady!   10

238 ❧

Con quai segni, signor, volete ch'io
vi mostri l'amor mio,
se, amando e morendo ad ora ad ora,
non si crede per voi, lassa, ch'io mora?
Aprite lo mio cor, ch'avete in mano,
e, se l'imagin vostra non v'è impressa,
dite ch'io non sia dessa;
e, s'ella v'è, a che pungermi invano
l'alma di sí crudi ami
con dir pur ch'io non v'ami?
Io v'amo ed amerò fin che le ruote
girin del sol, e piú, se piú si puote;
e, se voi nol credete,
è perché crudo sète.

238 ⅔

Tell me, my lord, by what sign I can show
My faithful love to you?
What though I love and die from hour to hour,
You still do not believe that I am dying.
Open my heart – you hold it in your hand –   5
And if your image is not printed there,
Say, I am not myself.
But if it is, why do you stab so vainly
My soul with such sharp hooks?
Saying I do not love you?   10
I love and I shall love you, while the spheres
Turn round the sun, and more if it could be.
If you do not believe me
This shows that you are cruel.

241 ❧

Donne, voi che fin qui libere e sciolte
degli amorosi lacci vi trovate,
onde son io e son tant'altre avolte,
  se di saper che cosa sia bramate
quest'Amor, che signor ha fatto e dio
non pur la nostra, ma l'antica etate,
  è un affetto ardente, un van disio
d'ombre fallaci, un volontario inganno,
un por se stesso e 'l suo bene in oblio,
  un cercar suo malgrado con affanno
quel che o mai non si trova, o, se pur viene,
avuto, arreca penitenzia e danno,
  un nutrir la sua vita sol di spene,
un aver sempre mai pensieri e voglie
di fredda gelosia, di dubbi piene,
  un laccio che s'allaccia e non si scioglie,
quando altrui piace, un gir spargendo seme,
di cui buon frutto mai non si ricoglie,
  una cura mordace, che 'l cor preme,
un la sua libertate e la sua gioia
e la sua pace andar perdendo insieme,

241 ࿐

Young ladies, you who still enjoy your freedom
    From the constraining bonds that Love imposes,
    With which I and so many more are bound,
If you wish passionately to have knowledge
    About this Love, who is made god and master   5
    Not only by this age, but by old times;
It is a burning feeling, vain desire
    For empty shadows, self-imposed deception,
    Setting your own well-being in disregard;
Seeking, despite yourself, until exhaustion,   10
    That which you never find, or if you find it,
    Once had, it brings regrets and evil days;
Trying to feed your life with hoping only,
    With raising futile thoughts and vain desires,
    With chilling jealousy and crowding doubts;   15
A knot that binds your heart and can't be loosened,
    A wish to please another, only sowing
    Such seeds as in the end bear no good fruit;
A biting care, bringing on heart's oppression,
    A way of losing liberty and pleasure,   20
    And robbing you both of your youth and peace;

un morir, né sentir perché si moia,
un arder dentro d'un vivace ardore,
un esser mesta e non sentir la noia,
 un mostrar quel ch'uom chiude dentr' e fore.
un esser sempre pallido e tremante,
un errar sempre e non veder l'errore,
 un avilirsi al viso amato innante,
un esser fuor di lui franca ed ardita,
un non saper tener ferme le piante,
 un aver spesso in odio la sua vita
ed amar piú l'altrui, un esser spesso
or mesta e fosca, or lieta e colorita,
 un ogni studio in non cale aver messo,
un fugir il comerzio de le genti,
un esser da sé lunge ed altrui presso,
 un far seco ragioni ed argomenti
e disegni ed imagini, che poi
tutti qual polve via portano i venti,
 un non dormire a pieno i sonni suoi,
un destarsi sdegnosa ed un sognarsi
sempre cosa contraria a quel che vuoi,
 un aver doglia e non voler lagnarsi
di chi n'offende, anzi rivolger l'ira
contra se stesso e sol seco sdegnarsi,
 un veder sol un viso ove si mira,
un in esso affissarsi, benché lunge,
un gioir l'alma, quando si sospira,
 e finalmente un mal che unge e punge.

A kind of death, not knowing why you're dying;
   An inward burning with a vivid flame,
   A sad existence, feeling no true grief;
Display of what were better kept in hiding,   25
   A way of life forever pale and trembling,
   Wandering in a way not understood;
Debasing of yourself toward the beloved,
   But when away from him, bold and defiant –
   Not knowing surely where to set your feet;   30
A state of holding your own life in hatred,
   Loving another more; your own existence
   Darkened and sad; again, happy and bright.
An apathy toward other occupations,
   Fleeing from company of other people;   35
   Close to one only, alien to yourself;
A constant inward arguing, discussion,
   Bringing up plans and images that later
   Turn into dust that the wind blows away;
A restless sleeping, never satisfying,   40
   Waking unhappy, still obsessed by dreaming
   Of things opposed to your own deeper will;
Though hurt, unable to express your grievance
   To the offender; misdirected anger
   Against yourself, disprizing of yourself;   45
Seeing one face alone that's worth the looking;
   Preoccupied with it, though at a distance;
   An inner happiness expressed in sighs –
   And finally, an ill that heals and wounds.

250 ❧

Voi n'andaste, signor, senza me dove
il gran troian fermò le schiere erranti,
ov'io nacqui, ove luce vidi innanti
dolce sí, che lo star mi spiace altrove.
   Ivi vedrete vaghe feste e nove,
schiere di donne e di cortesi amanti,
tanti, che ad onorar vengono, e tanti,
un de li dèi piú cari al vero Giove.
   Ed io, rimasa qui dov'Adria regna,
seguo pur voi e 'l mio natio paese
col pensier, ché non è chi lo ritegna.
   Venir col resto il mio signor contese;
ché, senza ordine suo, ch'io vada o vegna
non vuole Amor, poi che di lui m'accese.

250 ❧

Without me, lord, you went where the great Trojan
Stopped with his wandering hordes, where I was
    born,
Where the first light of heaven struck my eyes,
So sweet a place, none other is its equal.
There you will see the most delightful feasts,   5
Bevies of ladies and of courteous lovers,
And many pilgrims honoring that god,
Dearest of all the gods to the true Zeus.
And I am left where Adriatic reigns.
I follow you in thought to my dear birthplace,   10
My thought is unrestrained, but my departure
Was vetoed by my lord, without whose leave
Love does not let me go or come, since I
Was kindled with this all-consuming flame.

258

Signor, da poi che l'acqua del mio pianto,
che sí larga e sí spessa versar soglio,
non può rompere il saldo e duro scoglio
del cor del fratel vostro tanto o quanto,
    vedete voi, cui so ch'egli ama tanto,
se, scrivendogli umíle un mezzo foglio,
per vincer l'ostinato e fiero orgoglio
di quel petto poteste aver il vanto.
    Illustre Vinciguerra, io non disio
da lui, se non che mi dica in due versi:
— Pena, spera ed aspetta il tornar mio. —
    Se ciò m'aviene, i miei sensi dispersi,
come pianta piantata appresso il rio,
voi vedrete in un punto riaversi.

258 ❧

My lord, since all the waters of my weeping,
Which I pour out so freely and so often
Cannot break up the hard and solid rock
Which is your brother's heart, by much or little,
Plead now for me – I know he loves you dearly –   5
If, maybe writing humbly half a page,
You can defeat the obstinate, fierce pride
Within his breast, and thus achieve a triumph.
Illustrious Vinciguerra, I ask nothing
But that he tell me in a single couplet   10
To "Suffer, hope and wait for my return."
If that should happen, my distracted senses,
Like a dry tree replanted by a river,
Will be restored to health in little time.

270 ❧

Rivolgete la lingua e le parole
a dir di cosa più degna e più chiara,
che non son io, schiera onorata e cara,
onde tanto Elicona s'orna e cole.
     Come la luna il lume suo dal sole
prende, onde poi la notte apre e rischiara,
io, cui natura è stata in tutto avara,
splendo quanto il mio sol permette e vuole.
     A lui dunque si de' tutta la lode,
perché, s'ei non mi dá del suo vigore,
non è chi mova la mia lingua o snode.
     La mia vita in lui vive ed in me more,
di lui sol parla, pensa, scrive et ode.
Oh pur mi serbi in questo stato Amore!

270 ❧

Use all your eloquence to celebrate
One worthier and nobler far than I,
My dear and honorable group of friends
By whom the peak of Helicon is graced.
Just as the moon is lighted by the sun,   5
And with those rays reflected clears the night,
I, to whom Nature had been avaricious,
Glow with as much light as my sun allows.
So all your praise should be bestowed on him,
Since if he did not give me of his vigor,   10
No one could loosen or untie my tongue.
My life in him is living, dead in me,
It speaks, thinks, writes, and hears in him alone.
May Love keep me forever in this state.

276 🦢

Ben posso gir de l'altre donne in cima
fin dove il sole a noi nasce e diparte,
poi ch'io son scritta da le vostre carte,
Emo, e polita da la vostra lima.
    Il chiaro Achille ebbe la spoglia opima
d'onor fra gli altri gran figli di Marte,
non perché fusse tale egli in gran parte,
ma perché Omero lui alza e sublima.
    In me è sol amor, e disianza
di ber de l'acque del Castalio fiume,
ove voi spesso ed io ancor non fui.
    Se questo onesto mio disir s'avanza,
se un dí m'infonde Apollo del suo nume,
andrò lodando queste rive e vui.

276 ⪻

I can now count myself above all women
Between the sunrise and its setting point,
Since I have been recorded in your poems,
Emo, and polished by your artist's file!
Famous Achilles, who won such great spoils   5
Of honor, more than any son of Mars,
Attained his fame, not only for his deeds,
But because Homer raised him to such heights.
In me are only love and great desire
Of deeply drinking the Castalian waters,   10
Which you have drunk before, but I not yet;
And if this earnest wish of mine succeeds,
And if Apollo pours his gifts upon me,
I will go praising you and that high spring.

283 ❧

S'io non avessi al cor giá fatto un callo
e patteggiato dentro col pensiero
non dar piú luogo al despietato arciero,
mal trattata da lui quanto egli sallo;
   di farmi entrar ne l'amoroso ballo
novamente, e piú crudo che 'l primiero,
per farmi uscir dal mio preso sentiero
e commetter del primo un maggior fallo,
   avrian forza i vostr'occhi e quel cortese
atto e tante altre grazie e la beltade,
onde natura a farsi onor intese.
   Ma, per aver di me giusta pietade,
tanto ho di voi, non piú, le voglie accese,
quanto permette onor ed onestade.

283 ❧

If I had not hardened my heart already,
And made a treaty with my inmost mind
No longer to permit the cruel archer
– Who so mistreated me, as he well knows –
To make me join him in the dance of love   5
Another time, more fiercely than the first,
And make me stray from my well-chosen path,
Committing now a worse sin than before.
Your eyes, your gracious courtesy, your beauty,
Which nature gave you to enhance her pride,   10
Would have the power to sway me to your side.
But, to show rightful pity to myself,
I let my heart be kindled in your favor
Only within my honor's firm restraint.

298

Felice in questa e piú ne l'altra vita
chi fugge, come voi, prima che provi,
la miseria del secolo infinita;
   prima che dentr'al cor si turbi e movi
per tanti inaspettati uman cordogli,
e poi d'uscirne al fin loco non trovi.
   Felice anima, tu, che qui ti spogli
di questi affetti miseri e terreni,
e de le nostre pene non ti dogli!
   Tutti i tuoi dí saran lieti e sereni,
senz'ira, senza guerra e senza danni,
di pace, di riposo e d'amor pieni.
   Felice chi si fa, sotto umil panni,
di Cristo, signor suo, devot'ancella,
né prova i nostri maritali affanni!
   E, gli occhi alzando a la divina stella,
lascia quest'aspro e periglioso mare,
ch'aura giamai non ha senza procella!
   Felice chi non ha tant'ore amare,
né sente tutto 'l dí pianti e lamenti
o di troppo volere, o poco fare!

298 ᴢ

Happy in this life, happier in the next
Is she who flees, like you, before she tastes
The misery of living in this world,
   Before her heart is moved and deeply stirred
By all the unexpected human sorrows   5
From which she cannot find how to escape.
   A happy soul are you, who have stripped off
Our pains, and do not need to weep for them,
These wretched passions of our earthly life.
   All of your days will be serene and happy,   10
No anger, never warfare, never losses,
Filled full of peace, of rest, and quiet love.
   Happy is she, who dressed in humble garb,
Becomes the handmaid of our Lord, of Christ,
And never feels the pains of married life.   15
   Raising her eyes up to the Holy Star,
She leaves behind this perilous wild sea
Which never feels a breeze without a tempest.
   Happy is she who knows no bitter hours
And never hears the crying and complaints: 20
"She wants too much!" "She never does enough!"

Qui s'odon sol al fin con gran tormenti
o querele di figli o di consorte,
e mai de l'esser tuo non ti contenti.
  Infelice colei, ch'a questa sorte
chiama la trista sua disaventura,
ch'in vita sa che cosa è inferno e morte!
  Questa è una valle lagrimosa e scura,
piena d'ortiche e di pungenti spine,
dove il tuo falso ben passa e non dura.
  Infelici noi povere e meschine,
serve di vanitá, figlie del mondo,
lontane, aimè, da l'opre alte e divine!
  Altre per far il crin piú crespo e biondo
provan ogn'arte e trovan mille ingegni,
onde van de l'abisso l'alme al fondo.
  Infelice quell'altra move a' sdegni
il marito o l'amante, e s'affatica
di tornar grata e far che lei non sdegni.
  Ad altri piú che a se medesma amica,
quella con acque forti il viso offende,
de la salute sua propria nimica.
  Infelice colei, che sol attende
da mezzo dí, da vespro e da mattina,
e tutto 'l giorno a la vaghezza spende;
  per parer fresca, bianca e pellegrina
dorme senza pensar de la famiglia,
e negli empiastri notte e dí s'affina!

On earth, one feels so many kinds of torments,
Quarrels of children, angry words of husbands –
Never is one contented with her life.

    Unhappy she, whom sad misfortune calls   25
To such a fate! For in this way of life
She learns the meaning of both death and hell.

    This is a vale of tears and utter darkness,
Full of sharp nettles and of stinging thorns,
Where fleeting happiness will not endure.   30

    Unhappy ones are we, wretched and sad,
Vanity's slaves, we women of the world,
So distant from the noble works of God!

    Some strive to make their hair curly and blond,
Try every art, every ingenious trick   35
Which only drives their souls to the abyss.

    Unhappy this one, who provokes to anger
Her husband or her lover – then takes pains
To win him back so that he won't reject her.

    Wanting more to please others than herself,   40
One spoils her face with acids and bleaches,
Injuring in this way her own good health.

    Unhappy she, who spends both night and day,
Morning and evening, taking endless pains
On nothing else besides her own adornment.   45

    And one, to seem forever young and fresh,
Sleeps all day long, her family forgotten,
Smears ointments on her face both night and day.

Infelice quest'altra de la figlia
grande, che per voler darle marito,
senza quietar giamai, cura si piglia!

E, perché al mondo ha perso l'appetito,
non fa se non gridar, teme e sospetta
de l'onor suo che non gli sia rapito.

Infelice qualunque il frutto aspetta
de' cari figli, e sta con questa speme,
lagrimando cosí sempre soletta!

Questo l'annoia poi, l'aggrava e preme,
che misera da lor vien disprezzata,
e di continuo ne sospira e geme.

Infelice chi sta sempre arrabbiata,
e col consorte suo non ha mai posa,
mesta del tutto, afflitta e sconsolata!

Tropp'accorta al suo mal, vive gelosa,
e col figliuolo suo spesso s'adira,
non gusta cibo mai, mai non riposa.

Infelice quell'altra, che sospira,
ché sa che 'l suo marito poco l'ama,
e di mal occhio per mal far la mira!

Alcuna in testimonio il cielo chiama,
che sa di non aver commesso errore,
e pur talor si duol de la sua fama.

Infelice via piú chi porta amore,
e di vane speranze e van desiri
si va pascendo il tormentato core !

Another one worries about her daughter,
A grown girl, now to find her a good husband,   50
She never rests, taking this so to heart.
    And one has lost all pleasure in the world;
She cries all day, fearful and apprehensive
That she might somehow lose her reputation.
    Unhappy she, who dotes upon her children,   55
Expecting, hoping, they'll return her love.
She cries all day because she's left alone.
    This pains her then, and weighs upon her spirits;
Poor thing! Always neglected by them now,
She weeps and wails on this account all day.   60
    Another's always angry with her husband,
She's not at peace, even when he's at home,
Unhappy all the time, in her affliction.
    She knows the cause too well – it's jealousy!
And she is also angry with her son,   65
Till she can't eat, can't get a good night's rest.
    Another sighs… her husband does not love her.
She's sad because she knows how very little.
He, in his guilt, looks on her with distaste.
    Another calls on heaven to bear witness   70
That she has never done an evil deed –
Yet without cause, her honor has been blemished.
    Still more unhappy is the one who loves
And broods on fruitless hopes, with vain desires
Forever feeding her tormented heart.   75

Altre pene infinite, altri martíri,
che narrar non si sanno, il mondo apporta,
mill'altre angosce e mill'altri sospiri.
    Felice per seguir piú fida scorta
chi elegge di Maria la miglior parte,
e si fa viva a Cristo, al mondo morta!
    Felice chi sue voglie ha volte e sparte
al sommo Sole, al ben del paradiso,
e qui con umiltá pon cura ed arte!
    A voi convien, che 'l bel leggiadro viso
celate sotto puro e bianco velo,
avere il cor da uman pensier diviso.
    Felice voi, che, d'amoroso zelo
accesa, v'aggirate al vero Sole,
che luce eternamente in terra e 'n cielo!
    Voi correte qua giú rose e viole,
sará del viver vostro il fin beato,
ch'altro non è di chi tal vita vuole.
    Felice voi, che avete consacrato
i vaghi occhi divini, il bel crin d'oro
a chi sí bella al mondo v'ha creato!
    È questo il ricco, il caro e bel tesoro,
quest'è la preziosa margherita,
onde, di palme al fin cinta e d'alloro,
    vittoria porterete a Cristo unita.

How many other pains, infinite griefs
That no one could describe, grow in the world!
Thousands of anguishes, thousands of sighs!
    Happy are you who walk a path more sure,
who chose the better part that Mary chose,   80
and live in Christ but to the world are dead.
    Happy are you, who turn your every thought
Up to the highest Sun, to paradise,
And humbly give your thoughts and cares to God.
    How right you are to hide your lovely face   85
Beneath a spotless veil of purest white,
And keep your heart untouched by human cares!
    Happy are you, aflame with loving zeal,
Turning completely to the one true Sun
Which shines eternally on earth and heaven.   90
    Cloistered, you gather violets and roses.
You can look forward to a happy death:
None other comes to one who lives your life.
    Happy are you, you who have consecrated
Your lovely eyes to heaven, your gold hair   95
To Him who gave you beauty on the earth.
    This is the beautiful, the priceless treasure,
This is the precious pearl of which we read;
So, crowned in heaven with the palm and laurel,
    You will be joined by Christ in victory.   100

307 &

     — *Volgi a me, peccatrice empia, la vista* —
mi grida il mio Signor che 'n croce pende;
e dal mio cieco senso non s'intende
la voce sua di vera pietá mista,
     sí mi trasforma Amor empio e contrista,
e d'altro foco il cor arde ed accende;
sí l'alma al proprio e vero ben contende,
che non si perde mai, poi che s'acquista.
     La ragion saria ben facile e pronta
a seguire il suo meglio; ma la svia
questa fral carne, che con lei s'affronta.
     Dunque apparir non può la luce mia,
se 'l sol de la tua grazia non sormonta
a squarciar questa nebbia fosca e ria.

307 ?❧

"Turn now your eyes on me, you impious sinner,"
My Lord upon His cross cries out to me;
But still my blinded senses do not hear
His voice, mingled with pure and true compassion.
My foolish, worldly love has so transformed me,   5
That now my heart burns with a second flame.
My soul rebels against my own true good,
Which never can be lost, once it is won.
Reason, indeed, is ready and prepared
To tread the better way, but it is swayed   10
By this frail flesh contending with the right.
Therefore true Light cannot appear to me,
Unless Your Grace, O God, can overcome
And tear away this dark and evil cloud.

308 ❧

Purga, Signor, omai l'interno affetto
de la mia coscienzia, sí ch'io miri
solo in te, te solo ami, te sospiri,
mio glorioso, eterno e vero obietto.
    Sgombra con la tua grazia dal mio petto
tutt'altre voglie e tutt'altri disiri;
e le cure d'amor tante e i sospiri,
che m'accompagnan dietro al van diletto.
    La bellezza ch'io amo è de le rare
che mai facesti; ma, poi ch' è terrena,
a quella del tuo regno non è pare.
    Tu per dritto sentier lá su mi mena,
ove per tempo non si può cangiare
l'eterna vita in torbida, e serena.

308 ❧

Cleanse me, O Lord, from my internal passion
Which blinds my conscience still, that I may look
Only on You, love You alone, and sigh
Only for You, my true eternal Love.
Take with Your Grace from my encumbered heart   5
All other wishes, every wrong desire,
The many cares of love, the many sighs
That follow after every vain delight.
The beauty that I love is of the rarest
That ever You have made; yet it is earthly,   10
Not to compare with that of Your true kingdom.
You lead me on the better path above
Where nothing changes, nothing can be soiled
In that serene and everlasting life.

311 ❧

Mesta e pentita de' miei gravi errori
e del mio vaneggiar tanto e sí lieve,
e d'aver speso questo tempo breve
de la vita fugace in vani amori,
    a te, Signor, ch'intenerisci i cori,
e rendi calda la gelata neve,
e fai soave ogn'aspro peso e greve
a chiunque accendi di tuoi santi ardori,
    ricorro; e prego che mi porghi mano
a trarmi fuor del pelago, onde uscire,
s'io tentassi da me, sarebbe vano.
    Tu volesti per noi, Signor, morire,
tu ricomprasti tutto il seme umano;
dolce Signor, non mi lasciar perire!

311 ❧

Sad and repenting of my grievous errors
And of my frivolous and hollow straying,
Having misspent the little time allowed
For this brief life of ours, in empty loves,
To You, O Lord, who soften hardened hearts   5
And warm the coldest of the ice-bound snows
And sweeten every rash and heavy burden
For those who will receive Your sacred fires,
I run, and pray You to extend Your hand
To draw me from this perilous sea, where I   10
Could never free myself, for all my striving.
You did for us poor mortals freely die,
You did redeem the entire human race.
O my dear Lord, I pray, let me not perish!

Notes to the Poems

Poem 1: In this thematic prelude to her *Rime*, Gaspara echoes Petrarch's beginning to his *Rime*, *"Voi ch' ascoltate in rime sparse il suono."* Lines 5. well-born (*bennato*): implies qualities of the heart as well as birth. 13. lord: Collaltino di Collalto.

Poem 2: Lines 1. Gaspara met Collaltino on Christmas Day, 1548. Again a Petrarchan echo (*Rime* 3): Petrarch fell in love with Laura on Holy Friday, 1327; Gaspara, with an obvious parallel, on Christmas Day. 5. lord: Collaltino. 11. Eternal Care: God, who made her worthy of such a noble love.

Poem 3: Lines 1. Ascrean: Mount Helicon, in Greek mythology, was the home of the Muses; called Ascrean, since it was near the town of Ascra, where the poet Hesiod grew up. 2. shepherd: Hesiod, one of the most famous ancient Greek poets, who lived about a century after Homer, and was second only to him in fame. 5. high hill (Collalto): the family name of her lover, Count Collaltino di Collalto. 6. planet: planets were supposed to bestow talent and other gifts on people born in the period of their rising or transiting. 9. shade: Collaltino's influence.

Poem 4: See note to Poem 3, Line 6. In Renaissance astrology the moon indicated mutability and coldness. This is the first allusion to Collaltino's cold and inconstant attitude toward the poetess.

Poem 5: Lines 4. Lord of Delos: Apollo. 13. dwelling: in winter, Collaltino would move back to his country estate.

Poem 7: Line 1. lord: Collaltino.

Poem 8: Lines 2. fire: her love for Collaltino. 5. flint: unusual way to describe the kindling of her amorous fire. 8. pain and pen: a pun also in Italian (*pena* and *penna*).

Poem 9: Lines 3. lord: Collaltino. 5. You: now she is addressing Collaltino directly.

Poem 13: Lines 2-3. From India to Mauretania: that is, from one hemisphere to the other.

Poem 17: Lines 8. him: Collaltino. 12. This poem is very famous for its daring, near-blasphemous tone.

Poem 18: Line 13. my sun: her lover.

Poem 21: Lines 1. I: the God of Love is speaking, acknowledging his incapacity to help her gain her beloved's love. 2. lord: Collaltino; here the praises of the belovèd, as often, assume panegyric proportions.

Poem 22: addressed to Collaltino.

Poem 26: Line 8. true light: Collaltino.

Poem 27: Line 1. good example of Renaissance poetic devices.

Poem 34: Lines 1. fair mother: Venus, the mother of Cupid, god of Love. 4. this: the poetess, herself. 13. my sun: Collaltino.

Poem 41: Lines 2. Hold you too: The poem is directed to Collaltino, berating him for his coldness. 10. Milo: ancient Greek athlete famous for his superhuman strength, fifth century BCE.

Poem 43: Line 2. lord: Collaltino.

Poem 47: Lines 5. her: death, represented as feminine in Italian. 11. he: Collaltino. 13. sea: Gaspara is in Venice, therefore it is the Adriatic Sea. 14. hills: the hills of Collalto, Collaltino's estate.

Poem 49: Line 5. two faithful companions: Collaltino's eyes.

Poem 55: Line 6. fairest: Collaltino; First Care: God.

Poem 56: Line 7. North Star: the star used by ancient sailors to find direction, a metaphor for her lover.

Poem 64: Line 13. noble: in Italian "noble" means both by birth and character.

Poem 68: Line 1. "*Chiaro e famoso mare*" echoes Petrarch's famous canzone, "*Chiare fresche e dolci acque*" (*Rime* 126, Line 1): the sea is, of course, the Adriatic.

Poem 82: Lines 1. lagoon: Gaspara is in Venice. 2. Anaxilla: Gaspara took the literary name of Anaxilla, from the river Piave (in Latin, *Anaxus*), which flowed through Collalto. 5. shore: Collaltino is in France, on the Atlantic Ocean.

Poem 87: Lines 11. one: God, or the love of God. 13. by you: by Love. 14. source: Collaltino.

Poem 92: Lines 7. lights: her lover's eyes. 14. sun: her lover.

Poem 95: This poem is a sestina. Lines 1. sun: Collaltino. 37. O living sun: God.

Poem 97: Lines 1. courteous knight: Collaltino. 12. king: Henry II of France.

Poem 100: Lines 2. joy: Collaltino has written that he is coming back from France. 4. Lights: Collaltino's eyes.

Poem 101: Lines 3. Who now returns: Collaltino has announced his return from France. 4. sun...sole: pun in the Italian: *Sole* (sun) and *sol'* (sole).

Poem 102: Lines 3. he: Collaltino. 6. Collaltino has returned from the war in France. 8. Trebbia and Trasimene: famous bloody battles in ancient times between Rome and Carthage; Gaspara is here making a parallel to the present wars, which repeatedly kept her lover away from her.

Poem 104: Line 10. Alcmena: wife of Amphitryon, was loved by Zeus, who took the shape of her husband to spend the night with her. Zeus made this last night last as long as two ordinary ones, and the child begotten was Heracles.

Poem 111: In this poem the poet shows off her knowledge of classical poetry by echoing themes from Horace (*Odes* 1.22, ll. 17-24) and from Petrarch's *Rime* (Sonnet 145, "*Pommi ove 'l sole occide i fiori e l'erbe.*" Line 13. stars: her lover's eyes.

Poem 114: Line 5. he: Petrarch, whose love for Laura unfolded itself on French soil, where the rivers Sorga and Gebenna flow.

Poem 117: Line 1. waste: while Gaspara is seemingly telling Collaltino not to waste his time in praising her, in reality she is hinting that he should not waste time in writing poetry at all. In fact, he also wrote poetry, but of a very mediocre quality.

Poem 125: Line 12. lights: Collaltino's eyes; again, the tone is panegyric.

Poem 126: Lines 3. light: her lover. 13. When Collaltino reappears. 14. She becomes happy again, after her former sadness.

Poem 129: Line 4. sin: Collaltino, tired of the relationship, attempted to break it, blaming her for imaginary, it would seem, infidelities.

Poem 132: Lines 4. he: referring to Love. 6. him: referring to Collaltino; both: her heart and soul.

Poem 133: Lines 7. sands: meaning the aridity of her own life. 11. Gaspara means that she cannot commit suicide, because, metaphorically speaking, she is already without life, that is, without her love.

Poem 135: Because of the density and compactness of the Italian original, the English version did not fit within the standard fourteen-verse sonnet. Therefore, it was translated as a *sonetto caudato* – that is, a sonnet with a tail – and one more verse was added to the English to keep the sense of the original text. Lines 2. sea: the Adriatic Sea – Gaspara is in Venice, while Collaltino is in his Collalto estate. 5. hill: Collalto, "high hill," from which the noble family took its name. 8. name: Gaspara liked to call herself by the literary name Anaxilla, from the river Piave, in Latin *Anaxus*, which flowed through the Collalto estate; who: the river, the hill, the forest etc. 13. mirror of my heart: Collaltino.

Poem 136: Lines 5. when Collatino leaves. 10. addressing Collaltino directly.

Poem 139: Lines 1. Actually, the other way around. Gaspara took the literary name Anaxilla, from the river Piave, in Latin *Anaxus*, which flowed through the Collalto estate. 2. high hill: Collalto. 3. beech: symbol of the Collalto family; Collaltino is a noble branch of that tree. 8. Gaspara is extending the image: she competes with the river for the "shade," that is, the presence of Collaltino. She wanted him to stay in Venice with her, but the affairs of his estate and family kept him at Collalto. 11. The river, and by extension the whole estate, would keep Collaltino away from her when he had to leave Gaspara in Venice to attend to estate matters.

Poem 145: Lines 1. O happy country: the Collalto estate. 3. he: Collaltino. 8. Ancient Roman gods and demi-gods. 10. Collaltino is now living at his country estate.

Poem 146: Lines 2. he: referring to Collaltino. 5. hill: Collaltino is now at Collalto, "high hill," his estate. 10. beauty: Collaltino's beauty; Gaspara is in Venice. 13. Anaxilla: poetic name for Gaspara, after the river Piave, *Anaxus*, flowing through Collaltino's lands. 14 lights: Collaltino's eyes.

Poem 147: Line 8. The activities of war and intellectual pursuits.

Poem 150: Lines 1. She is addressing directly her tears and her burning pain. 10. low-born: she is very aware of the difference in the social status between her and her lover. 12. each: she and Collaltino.

Poem 151: Lines 2. He: Collaltino. 8. Gaspara's poetic epitaph for herself is strangely prophetic.

Poem 152: Lines 3. him: Collaltino. 10. sun: Collaltino. 13. him: Collaltino.

Poem 155: Line 14: Gaspara hopes to die before seeing Collaltino in love with another.

Poem 161: Lines 1. nest: Collaltino's castle, where she had lived for a while with him. 7. She had returned to her home in Venice.

Poem 164: Line 10. lord: Collaltino.

Poem 166: Lines 10: Gaspara is very conscious of the difference in social status between her and the object of her love. 14. high fire: for Phaethon and Icarus the sun; for the poetess, a man of a much higher social rank, Collaltino.

Poem 167: Lines 5. evil one: Collaltino. 9. my harm: Collaltino's infidelity.

Poem 172: Line 10. recompense: requited love.

Poem 174: Line 12. Chimera: fire-breathing monster from Greek mythology.

Poem 175: Line 1. Collaltino is about to leave for France.

Poem 179: Line 8. Gordian knot: a knot said to be impossible to unfasten, except by the conqueror of Asia; the legend says that Alexander the Great solved the dilemma by expeditiously cutting it with his sword.

Poem 197: Line 9. one: Collaltino.

Poem 199: Line 3. Collaltino is about to go to France, to distinguish himself in war.

Poem 202: Line 3. eyes: Collaltino's eyes. 5. Sun: God. 14. One: God.

Poem 208: Lines 2. salamander: a mythical creature who could only live in fire. 3. bird of fable: the phoenix. 6. The great twentieth-century Italian poet Gabriele D'Annunzio chose this verse as his motto.

Poem 209: Lines 1. She first met Collaltino on Christmas Day (note the analogy to Petrarch's *Rime* (3): Petrarch met Laura at Easter time, on Holy Friday). 13. Sense: here meant as sensuality.

Poem 210: Lines 2. new arrow: she is about to fall in love again. 3. first wound: her unrequited love for Collaltino. 5. his fire: the fire of Love; her propensity for falling in love. 8. from him: from Love.

Poem 211: Lines 6. Gaspara is about to fall in love for the second time. 9. He: Love, compared to an archer.

Poem 214: Lines 1. wound: her love for Collaltino; she is falling in love again with another man, but she is afraid. 6. Refers to Christ's wounds.

Poem 216: Lines 10. lord: Collaltino. 12. his: Collaltino's. 13. sweetness: meaning that he might love her again. 14. She has now become almost impervious to pain.

Poem 221: Lines 7. it: she is referring either to a new dawn of hope or to a new lover. 9. She has mixed feelings about the new love.

Poem 230: Lines 2-3. Collaltino had complained that she had not shed tears when he left.

Poem 232: Lines 9. strange beast: the salamander, a mythical animal who lived only in fire. 13. Often quoted as an example of Gaspara's *voluptas dolendi*, or pleasure in being hurt.

Poem 235: Line 1. Count: Collaltino di Collalto.

Poem 241: This is a narrative poem in *terza rima,* warning women against love and its evils.

Poem 250: Lines 1. lord: Gaspara is addressing herself to a lord, other than Collaltino, who had invited her to go with him on a trip to her natal town of Padua; according to an old tradition, a group of refugees from the Trojan War settled in a place later called Padua, under the leadership of Antenor. 7. Following a common Renaissance style, the word "god" is here used for a "saint," in this case St. Anthony of Padua. 8. The true Zeus is the Christian God. 9. Gaspara is in Venice at this time. 12. lord: Collaltino.

Poem 258: Lines 1. lord: the sonnet is addressed to Vinciguerra II, Collaltino's brother, asking him to plead for her. 10. he: Collaltino himself.

Poem 270: Lines 2. one: Collaltino. 3. group of friends: group of poets, friends of Gaspara. 4. Helicon: mountain sacred to Apollo and to the Muses. 8. sun: Collaltino again.

Poem 276: Lines 4. Leonardo Emo: a contemporary poet who wrote in praise of her and gave her poetic advice; file: from Horace, *Ars Poetica*: "Do not neglect the labors of the file." 6. son of Mars: warrior. 10. Castalia was a mountain spring near Delphi, believed to make anyone who drank its waters a poet. 14: spring: Castalia again.

Poem 283: Lines 3. cruel archer: Love. 6. another time: she is afraid she will fall in love again. 9. your: she is addressing the man who is wooing her, possibly G. A. Guiscardo or Viscardo.

Poem 298: Lines 2. you: this poem in *terza rima* is dedicated to a nun, Suor Angelica Paolo, who exerted a profound religious influence on Gaspara. 16: Holy Star: God. 26: fate: the state of marriage. 41. acids and bleaches: blond hair and a very white complexion were the fashion of the day. 95. pearl: Matt. 43:46: parable of the man who sold all his goods in order to purchase one precious pearl, i.e., the love of God.

Poem 307: Lines 7. true good: love of God. 11. right: salvation. 14. dark and evil cloud: carnal desire.

Poem 308: Line 9: beauty: Collaltino.

BIBLIOGRAPHY

EDITIONS

Rime di Madonna Gaspara Stampa. Ed. Cassandra Stampa with Giorgio Benzone. Venice: Plinio Pietrasanta, 1554.

Rime di Madonna Gaspara Stampa con alcune altre di Collaltino e di Vinciguerra conti di Collalto, e di Baldassarre Stampa. Ed. Luisa Bergalli with Apostolo Zeno. Venice: Piacentini, 1738.

Rime di Gaspara Stampa. Biographical essay by Pia Mestica Chiappetti. Florence: Barbera, 1877.

Rime di tre gentildonne del secolo XVI: Vittoria Colonna, Gaspara Stampa, Veronica Gambara. Ed. Olindo Guerrini. Milan: Sonzogno, 1883.

Rime di Gaspara Stampa e di Veronica Franco. Ed. Abelkader Salza. Bari: Laterza, 1913.

Le più belle pagine di Gaspara Stampa, Vittoria Colonna, Veronica Gambara, Isabella di Morra. Ed. Giuseppe Toffanin. Milan: Treves, 1935.

Rime. Ed. Rodolfo Ceriello. Milan: Rizzoli, 1954; new ed. 1976 with intro. by Maria Bellonci.

SECONDARY SOURCES

Baldacci, Luigi. "Gaspara Stampa." In *Lirici del Cinquecento.* Florence: Salani, 1957, 102-8.

——. *Il Petrarchismo italiano nel '500.* Padua: Liviana, 1964.

Bandini Buti, M. "Gaspara Stampa," *Poetesse e scrittrici.* In *Enciclopedia biografica e bibliografica italiana,* ser. 4, pt. 6. Milan: Istituto editoriale italiano (Tosi), 1941, 2:278-83.

Barzaghi, Antonio. *Donne o cortegiane? La prostituzione a Venezia. Documenti di costume dal XVI al XVII secolo.* Verona: Bertani, 1980.

Bassanese, Fiora. "A Feminine Voice: Gaspara Stampa." *Canadian Journal of Italian Studies* 3, 2 (1980): 81-88.

—. *Gaspara Stampa.* Boston: Twayne, 1983.

—. "Gaspara Stampa's Poetics of Negativity." *Italica* 61 (1984): 335-46.

Bellonci, Maria. "La vita e gli amori della poetessa padovana Gaspara Stampa." *Supplemento del Corriere della Sera*, Sept. 26, 1976.

Benson, Pamela. *The Invention of the Renaissance Woman: The Challenge of Female Independence in the Literature and Thought of Italy and England.* University Park: Pennsylvania State University Press, 1992.

Binni, Walter. "Gaspara Stampa." In *Critici e poeti dal Cinquecento al Novecento.* Florence: La Nuova Italia, 1951, 3-16.

Bo, Carlo. *Lirici del Cinquecento.* Milan: Garzanti, 1941, 43-51, 297-331.

Bonora, Ettore. "Le donne poetesse." In *Critica e letteratura nel Cinquecento.* Turin: Giappichelli, 1964, 93-110.

Brognolino, Gioacchino. "Gaspara Stampa." *Giornale storico della letteratura italiana* 76 (1920): 134-45.

Calcaterra, Carlo. "Il Petrarca e il Petrarchismo." In *Questioni e correnti di storia letteraria.* Ed. Attilio Momigliano. Problemi ed orientamenti critici di lingua e letteratura italiana, 3. Milan: Marzorati, 1949.

Casagrande di Villaviera, Rita. *Le cortegiane veneziane nel Cinquecento.* Milan: Longanesi, 1968.

Cesareo, Giovanni Alfredo. *Gaspara Stampa, donna e poetessa.* Naples: Perrella, 1920.

Costa-Zalessow, Natalia. *Scrittrici italiane dal XIII al XX secolo: Testi e critica.* Ravenna: Longo, 1982.

Croce, Benedetto. "Gaspara Stampa nell'immaginazione, Gaspara Stampa nella realtà, Estetismo astratto a proposito di Gaspara Stampa." In *Conversazioni critiche.* Ser. 2. Bari: Laterza, 1924, 223-33.

De Benedetti, F. A. "La poesia di Gaspara Stampa." *Rassegna nazionale* ser. 3, 34 (1936): 210-16.

De Blasi, Jolanda. *Antologia delle scrittrici italiane dalle origini al 1800.* Florence: Nemi, 1930.

Dolci, Giulio. "Gaspara Stampa." In *Letteratura Italiana: I Minori.* Milan: Marzorati, 1961, 2:1315-25.

Donadoni, Eugenio. *Gaspara Stampa: Vita e opere.* Messina: Principato, 1919.

Einstein, Alfred. *The Italian Madrigal.* Princeton: Princeton University Press, 1971.

Flora, Francesco. *Gaspara Stampa e altre poetesse del '500.* Milan: Nuova Accademia, 1962.

Greer, Germaine. *The Obstacle Race: The Fortunes of Women Painters and Their Work.* New York: Farrar, Straus, Giroux, 1979.

Innocenzi Gregio, Elisa. "In difesa di Gaspara Stampa." *Ateneo Veneto* 38, 1 (1915): 1-160, 280-99.

Jones, Ann Rosalind. "Surprising Fame: Renaissance Gender Ideologies and Women's Lyric." In *The Politics of Gender.* Ed. Nancy K. Miller. New York : Columbia University Press, 1986.

—. *The Currency of Eros: Women's Love Lyric in Europe, 1540-1620.* Bloomington: Indiana University Press, 1990, 118-54.

—. "New Songs for the Swallow: Ovid's Philomela in Tullia d'Aragona and Gaspara Stampa." In *Refiguring Women: Gender Studies and the Italian Renaissance.* Ed. Marylin Migiel and Juliana Schiesari. Ithaca: Cornell University Press, 1991.

Jordan, Constance. *Renaissance Feminism: Literary Texts and Political Models.* Ithaca: Cornell University Press, 1990.

Kelly-Gadol, Joan. "Did Women Have a Renaissance?" In *Becoming Visible: Women in European History.* Ed. Renate Bridenthal and Claudia Koonz. Boston: Houghton Mifflin, 1977.

Labalme, Patricia H. *Beyond Their Sex: Learned Women of the European Past.* New York: New York University Press, 1980.

—. "Venetian Women on Women: Three Early Modern Feminists." *Archivio veneto,* ser. 5, 117 (1981): 81-109.

Larivaille, Paul. *La vie quotidienne des courtisanes en Italie au temps de la Renaissance.* Paris: Hachette, 1975.

Lawner, Lynne. *Lives of the Courtesans.* New York: Rizzoli, 1987.

—. "Gaspara Stampa and the Rhetoric of Submission." *Renaissance Studies in Honor of Craig Hugh Smith.* Ed. Andrew Morrogh et al. Harvard University, Villa I Tatti Publications 7. Florence: Giunti Barbera, 1985, 1:345-62.

Lenzi, Maria L. *Donne e madonne: L'educazione femminile nel primo rinascimento italiano.* Turin: Loescher, 1982.

Lipking, Lawrence. *Abandoned Women and Poetic Tradition.* Chicago: University of Chicago Press, 1988.

Logan, Oliver. *Culture and Society in Venice, 1470-1790.* New York: Scribner's, 1972.

Macchia, Giovanni. "Quattro poetesse del Cinquecento." *Rivista Rosminiana di filosofia e cultura* 31 (1937): 152-57.

Macina, Luisa Gervasio (pseud. Luigi di San Giusto). *Gaspara Stampa.* Bologna: Formiggini, 1909.

Malagoli, Luigi. *La lirica del Cinquecento e Gaspara Stampa.* Pisa: Editrice Goliardica, 1966.

—. "La nuova sensibilità e il nuovo stile: Gaspara Stampa." In *Le contraddizioni del Rinascimento.* Florence: La Nuova Italia, 1968, 105-23.

Masson, Georgina. *Courtesans of the Italian Renaissance.* New York: St. Martin's, 1976.

Migiel, Marylin and Juliana Schiesari, eds. *Refiguring Women: Gender Studies and the Italian Renaissance.* Ithaca: Cornell University Press, 1991.

Musatti, Eugenio. *La donna in Venezia.* Padua: Forni, 1992.

Neri, Ferdinando. "Le rime ultime di Gaspara Stampa." In *Saggi di letteratura italiana, francese e inglese.* Naples: Loffredo, 1936, 268-73.

Pancrazi, Pietro. "I due romanzi di Gasparina." In *Nel Giardino di Candido.* Florence: Le Monnier, 1950.

Pullan, Brian. *Rich and Poor in Renaissance Venice.* Cambridge, MA: Harvard University Press, 1971.

Reichenbach, Giulio. *L'altro amore di Gaspara Stampa.* Bologna: Zanichiello, 1907.

—. *Gaspara Stampa.* Rome: Formiggini, 1923.

Rilke, Rainer Maria. *The Selected Poetry.* Ed. and trans. Stephen Mitchell. New York: Vintage, 1989.

—. *The Notebooks of Malte Laurids Brigge.* Trans. Stephen Mitchell. New York: Vintage, 1985, 134, 235.

Rodocanachi, Emmanuel. *La femme italienne à l'èpoque de la Renaissance.* Paris: Hachette, 1907.

Rose, Mary Beth, ed. *Women in the Middle Ages and the Renaissance.* Syracuse: Syracuse University Press, 1986.

Rosenthal, Margaret. "Venetian Women Writers and Their Discontents." In *Sexuality and Gender in Early Modern Europe: Institutions, Texts, Images.* Ed. James Grantham Turner. Cambridge: Cambridge University Press, 1992.

Ruggieri, Guido. *The Boundaries of Eros: Sex Crime and Sexuality in Renaissance Venice.* Oxford: Oxford University Press, 1985.

Russo, Luigi. "Gaspara Stampa e il Petrarchismo del Cinquecento." *Belfagor* (Florence) 13 (Jan. 31, 1958): 1-20.

Salza, Abelkader. "Madonna Gasparina Stampa secondo nuove indagini." *Giornale storico della letteratura italiana* 62 (1913): 1-101.

—. "Madonna Gasparina Stampa e la società veneziana del suo tempo: nuove discussioni." *Giornale storico della letteratura italiana* 69-70 (1917).

Schiesari, Juliana. *The Gendering of Melancholia: Feminism, Psychoanalysis, and the Symbolics of Loss in Renaissance Literature.* Ithaca and London: Cornell University Press, 1992.

Servadio, Gaia. *La donna nel Rinascimento.* Milan: Garzanti, 1986.

Spiller, Michael E. G. *The Development of the Sonnet: An Introduction.* London and New York: Routledge, 1992.

Toffanin, Giuseppe. *Le donne poetesse e Michelangelo.* Milan: Vallardi, 1927.

—. *Il Cinquecento.* Milan: Vallardi, 1954.

Vassalli, Donati Chimenti. "Emancipazione e schiavitù in Gaspara Stampa." *Osservatore Politico Letterario* 19, 9 (1972): 70-85.

Ventura, Angelo. *Nobilità e popolo nella società veneta del '400 e '500.* Bari: Laterza, 1964.

Vitiello, Justin. "Gaspara Stampa: The Ambiguities of Martyrdom." *Modern Language Notes* 90 (1975): 58-71.

First-Line Index

*This Book Was Completed on September 19, 1994
At Italica Press, New York, New York and Was
Set in Garamond. It Was Printed on 50 lb
Natural Acid-Free Paper with
A Smyth-Sewn Binding by
McNaughton & Gunn,
Saline, MI
U. S. A.*

* *

*